Love Where You Live

CREATING EMOTIONALLY ENGAGING PLACES

By
Peter Kageyama

Illustrations by Michelle Royal

ISBN: 0692269347
ISBN 13: 9780692269343
Library of Congress Control Number: 2014918113
Creative Cities Productions

Acknowledgements

I have been fortunate to have spoken all over the world since the publication of my first book, *For the Love of Cities*, in 2011. People often tell me that my talks are inspirational, which is incredibly flattering. In truth, the people I meet and the projects and stories they share with me are the inspiration. I am the messenger. I tell their stories and pay it forward. I say to folks that when they share their story with me, I may share their story down the line and hopefully their work will inspire someone else to get in the game and do something for their community. This book is my way of paying forward all the great stories and projects people have shared with me over the past several years. Thank you!

Special thanks to the Community Foundation of Kalamazoo in Michigan. In 2012 I was invited to speak there and I also did a community workshop. While there they shared with me their annual report which was titled "Love Where You Live." They had tapped into the emotional connection people had for the community and were challenging donors to show their love by getting more involved. The name obviously stuck with me, so thank you very much Kalamazoo!

Personal thanks to: Michelle Royal, Charles Landry, Michelle Bauer, Rebecca Ryan, Giorgio Di Cicco, Larry Quick, Bob Devin Jones, Jane Cage, Andy Stoll, Amanda Styron, Chris Carey, Grant Tromp, Tracey Rudduck-Gudsell, Craig Christie, Jeff Vines, Randy Vines, Reuben Pressman, Hunter Payne, Stephanie Darden, T. Hampton Dohrman, Genci Xhelaj, Jen Wolters Cross, Bill Foster, Jeff Slobotski, Jack Storey, Heidi Sytsema, Bob Chapla, Jeanne Oakes, Chad Emerson, Vince Long, Greg Burris, Kristina Cooke, Jenny Oloman (J.O.), Peter Kenyon, Mike Lydon, Jeff Speck, Bill Given, Todd Bobiak, Tracy Willms Deane, Jennifer Thomas and my fabulous editor Megan Voeller. Thanks to those who have left us but continue to inspire and guide me: Paul Kageyama, Molly Moore, Gladys Hazen, Deanne Roberts and David Honeycutt.

Forward by Charles Landry

Cities are an emotional experience first and foremost. And certain emotions create energy and commitment from which motivation and the will to act then grows. This is when we engage. Many people have affection, pride for their city, but when this turns to love it activates the senses more deeply. Love then becomes a resource and it helps to make the best of what we have got, because it looks at things through positive eyes. Our love for where we live can make us determined and also impatient to get things done and not to be put off. Loving your city can make you frustrated which is why at times you must break the rules.

When you take an eagle eye view of cities around the world it is astonishing to note how love has been used as a regenerative focus. I am thinking here of Medellin in Colombia, once the murder capital of the world fuelled by drug money, that then used its love campaign to turn fear into hope. Or at the other extreme Helsinki where young activists initiated a raft of love inspired campaigns to bring the city to life including its citizen driven restaurant days where locals create restaurants in the streets, courtyards and parks. Initially forbidden the city then changed legislation to allow informal eating and this has had consequences for other areas too.

In great cities you sense a spirit of generosity visible in small gestures and the large and it is these that can make ordinary places extra-ordinary even if they are down at heel. Cities are complex and often it is the devotion of ordinary people that makes the difference.

This is where Peter Kageyama's *Love Where You Live* is so instructive. It gives us an excellent overview of what is possible. He has travelled widely looking at the odd, the inspiring and surprising and some projects he describes are really catalytic yet so easy and cheap to do. I particularly like Peter's own attitude which is always to take the glass half full approach in trying to harness the collective imagination of the people in the places he works. And finally his idea of the emotional caretaker of the city is something none of us should forget.

Charles Landry
September 9, 2014
Near Stroud, UK

For Michelle — Love is the best thing we do.

Introduction: Do You Love Where You Live?

It is easy to say you love your place. It is much harder to show it, in part because of the way we think about the nature of city building. We see that powerful leaders in government or business, or rich developers and corporations, build cities. We see ourselves as spectators to the process because it all seems so very big. We need to show people—everyday citizens—that they have a role to play. Citizens can't build roads, schools or waterfront parks. They cede this power to government and business. And what they can do, e.g., pop up festivals, yarn bombing, block cleanups and murals, is often seen as nice, or sweet, but not "serious" city building. Because of this, our own citizens don't believe in the importance of their small-scale efforts. Do not mistake small for unimportant. In our personal lives, it is often the small things, the tiny acts of love or neglect, which make or break relationships. Our radar is attuned to the big things in our cities and our relationships. We need to recalibrate that radar to see how important small, hyper-local and fun interventions are to the health and progress of our communities.

Over the past four years, I have seen the power of the small thing, the often silly and dismissible idea that makes people smile. There is game-changing power in these small things. Perhaps not in the first iteration, or even the second or third, but as citizens learn how to make things happen, they gain confidence and advance their ideas. Small aspirations become big, and a few iterations down the road, silly projects and their instigators may create a transformative project for a city. Even if they don't, along the way they will create experiences that make our cities better, more interesting and more lovable. What we build, we value. What we own, we cherish. When we see ourselves as builders, owners and active makers of our cities, even in the smallest ways, we are invested in our communities to a degree that a (metaphorical) "renter" or visitor is not.

My goal is to embolden those who believe emotions matter and show them how we can be intentional about cultivating such feelings within our communities. If you are a mayor, a council member, city manager, business leader or concerned citizen, this book will provide a starting point for your efforts. There is no prescriptive playbook for cultivating emotions, but some common threads have emerged from my experience, and I am pleased to be able to share them with you. In these examples, I hope you find an idea that clicks and that you will find the inspiration to make something happen in your backyard. We can all be city builders on some scale, but the first step in the process for most of us is to believe that we are capable of doing it and that we cannot and should not wait for permission to act.

Chapter One
Start Here

MARSHALL YOUR CO-CREATORS

In *For the Love of Cities,* I introduced the idea of "co-creators," those citizens who, often unofficially, are making their communities better, more interesting, more lovable places. These exceptional people make the content that we all consume, and places are much better for having these people active and engaged.

If you are a mayor, city manager, council member or some other type of community leader, you should be asking yourself: How do I work with these co-creators? How do I enlist their help in making a better community? These are challenging questions for municipal leaders because the answers don't fit the normal way we think about marshaling services. If you are a city leader and need volunteers, you have a well-established process for securing them. If you need to hire an outside consultant to do something for the city, you have a list of vendors, an RFQ or RFP process, and a hiring procedure. But you don't have anything like this for working with entrepreneurial co-creators who are self-motivated and largely working without official supervision. So we need some new guidelines.

FIRST STEPS:

1. Identify the anchor personas.

If I were the mayor or manager of my city, one of the first things I would do is to convene a meeting with my community's well-established co-creators. You know who these folks are—they are the easily identifiable community activists, social entrepreneurs and connectors who function as the big fish in the social pond of your place.

2. Bring these co-creators together.

The next step is to invite half a dozen of them to your office for a sit-down and a conversation. If asked to come to city hall to meet with the mayor, most citizens are going to feel flattered, or at least curious enough to accept the invitation. The cost to the city is an hour of your time and perhaps a cup of coffee!

3. Ask them for help.

Once you have them in your office, you are going to do something that is highly unusual. You, the city, are going to ask them, the citizen for their help. Usually it works the other way around, because historically the city has had the resources and the citizens would come in to ask for those resources. Now the city is seeking to tap into this new resource—the co-creators of its communities. Hopefully, if I am the co-creator being asked for help, I am flattered and curious enough to see how I might work with my city.

4. Amplify what they naturally do.

As the city, you need to remember a key point about these co-creators: You do not need to get them started. They are already out there doing things. You need to amplify what they are already doing. Starting something is difficult. It requires energy and resources. Amplifying something already in process is easier, but it requires a deft touch. You need to find ways to complement and add to the existing momentum. This means you will not be dictating the terms and conditions of the engagement, which may be the biggest difference and biggest challenge in this process.

5. Provide them with "other" resources.

The past several years have not been kind to city budgets. While there are positive signs on the horizon for cities and their finances, most still do not have additional funds to support co-creators with the sought-after resource of money. That is fine because you, the city, have all kinds of other resources. Resources include expertise and the ability to help navigate citizens through various departmental bureaucracies. You have the ability to provide police and fire service for events. You can waive some fees, such as Muskegon, Michigan, did for event permits so long as the event was part of their overall Love Muskegon campaign (described in Chapter Two), a flexible designation that was able to include many events.

Sometimes it is as simple as opening up the city's toy chest and allowing co-creators an opportunity to play with your toys. A great example comes from Dunedin, Florida, a small town not far from St. Petersburg, where I live. The parks and recreation department of Dunedin purchased an inflatable outdoor movie screen. The city uses it a handful of times a year for screenings, but for the vast majority of the time it sits in storage. Imagine making that resource available and asking your co-creative community what they might do with an outdoor movie screen. Backyard film festival anyone? Rooftop movie night? Best of all, the city does not own the project or have any responsibility beyond providing the screen.

After sharing this example, I once had a city leader ask me what happens if neo-Nazis want to use the movie screen? To which I replied, "Don't let them." I know the slippery slope arguments, and I also understand the First Amendment issue in the hypothetical sense. (I am a recovering attorney, after all.) But fear of a possible extreme situation should not be a reason for doing nothing and locking down all resources in bureaucracy and risk management-inspired rules. People have more common sense than we often give them credit for, and if the extreme situation does arise, you can deal with it then. In the meantime, you should encourage the creative and entrepreneurial spirit of your citizens and work with them to explore opportunities.

6. Ask them to identify more "lovers" of the city.

After bringing a group of co-creators together, I recommend that you invite them back a few months later to repeat the process. The next time you invite them back, ask them to bring a friend, a fellow co-creator who you may not have known. The co-creators in your community will have these other co-creators on their radar and will be the ones most likely to spot the up-and-coming individuals who you would definitely like to know moving forward.

7. Expand the circle.

If you start with half a dozen co-creators in the first meeting and invite them back with a friend in a few months and do that once again, in the space of three meetings and six to twelve months, you could have two dozen active co-creators who are engaged in some capacity with your city. Perhaps most importantly, these people will come to see the city as a partner in their work instead of an obstacle that must be overcome or avoided.

WOO YOUR CO-CREATORS

Greg Burris is the city manager of Springfield, Missouri. I met him at the state's annual gathering of city managers in 2013. What struck me about Burris is that he is not a classically trained city manager. In fact, he proudly says, "I'm an IT guy." But years of working in and around the city eventually earned him the city's top management position. I liked his untraditional perspective from the start. He also asked me interesting questions, including this one: How do we woo co-creators?

What I love about the question is that it starts from the right frame of mind. Burris might have asked, "How do we attract and retain our talented people?" or "How do we prevent brain drain?" But he didn't. He asked how do we "woo" them. Woo is a funny word that is not often used in the context of cities, but it is absolutely the right one when it comes to conversations with co-creators. As I wrote in *For the Love of Cities*, the co-creators in your community don't require your permission, your encouragement or even, for the most part, your resources. They are already out there doing things. The job of mayors, city council and city managers is to find ways to connect with them and work with them where possible, supporting their projects (which may mean staying out of their way) and trying to channel their efforts toward your long-term city vision. These co-creators will not take your orders, and they will think long and hard before accepting resources that have too many strings attached. Think of them as very talented free agents who have lots of options and do not need you in the way that you need them. In this power paradigm, cities would do well to remember the concept of "wooing" another person.

When we are out to win the love and affection of another person, we don't make logic-based, practical pitches as to the virtues of a relationship with us. If that were the case, you would hand out your resume, credit report and tax returns to the object of your affection. When we woo another person, we shift into a different mode that is all about feelings, desires, wish fulfillment and ego. Yes, ego. While these free agent co-creators are largely immune to your traditional pitch, they have egos just like everyone else.

The first step in the wooing process is to let them know that you're interested. How do you break the ice with co-creators? Just as in dating, it helps to have someone introduce you. I would recommend having those co-creators who you are already engaged with in some capacity provide an introduction to the extended co-creator community. This could be a simple as a cup of coffee or lunch, or as intentional as the process of marshaling co-creators that I outlined above. The best introduction will come from a member of the co-creative community with whom you are already acquainted.

A little ego stroking never hurts either. Let them know how much we value their efforts. Can you find ways to recognize their efforts, both old and new? A "Bob Devin Jones Day"—in honor of my friend and archetypal co-creator from St. Petersburg, Florida, who I highlighted in *For the Love of Cities*—may be a bit over the top, especially at the outset, but it is worth considering. To start, how about a simple shout-out on the city's or the mayor's Facebook page or Twitter feed? That is an easy place to begin.

From there, how about a personal visit to their workspace or project? When was the last time a mayor, council member or administrator dropped by the office or studio of one of the city's co-creators, just to see what cool new stuff they were working on? While you are there, you might consider inviting them to a council meeting to present their work to the broader leadership of the city—just something that would help the city get to know their co-creators better. Perhaps sometime in the future there will be funding available or a project that would be ideal for a collaborative partnership.

From there, think about the wooing process like dating. Find things that you can invite them to—perhaps something unexpected, such as an appropriate staff meeting. Look for ways to bring numbers of them together. Many cities now have their own TEDx events. Co-creators often make great speakers because they have interesting and relevant stories to tell the community. Once you begin to think about creating these relationships, you will find all kinds of ways to extend and deepen them. But you have to start with the idea of wooing the co-creators. And you, the traditional leadership of the city, have to make the first move. The co-creators think of you as either an obstacle to overcome or as irrelevant to their efforts. You need to convince them otherwise, and that means taking the first step.

If you're thinking this sounds a bit like matchmaking, you are correct. In his seminal book *The Rise of the Creative Class*, Richard Florida highlighted the economic imperative to attract talented people to our communities. Once there, they need to connect and plant roots in order to stay. One of Burris's next projects is based on the idea that Springfield should find ways to connect talented people to projects and organizations in need of help. Instead of the city providing direct resources, it will indirectly provide support by connecting talented people with places where they can make a difference in the community. Co-creators are a development resource that cities can use, but to tapping into them requires new ways of thinking about their role in the process and even playing the unusual role of matchmaker.

START A PHILANTHROPIC CULTURE

In *For the Love of Cities*, I posited that philanthropy, measured in numbers of grant making organizations per capita, was a way of measuring a community's giving spirit. As part of my assessment of lovable cities, philanthropy was one of the six key measures. In simple terms, a giving community is a lovable community because its members have a generous spirit and have learned to look beyond themselves to see the interconnectedness of all of the community's members. A philanthropic community is also indicative of a stable and successful region where people have achieved enough that they feel the need to give back. In creating my lists, I purposefully did not rank the amount of money granted back to the community, as this would have privileged older, more established communities that have philanthropic legacies dating back over a century. It would be unfair to compare the assets of the nearly one hundred-year old Cleveland Foundation, which has billions under management, with the Community Foundation of Tampa Bay, which is just twenty-three years old. Instead, I focused on the numbers of grant makers rather than the size of grants. More grant makers per capita indicated a more pervasive philanthropic culture.

There are more than 1,400 community foundations worldwide, with over half of them in the United States. Every U.S. state has at least one community foundation. Add to that number other, nationally recognized philanthropic groups such as the United Way, private foundations and faith-based foundations, and you have a remarkable network of giving. Some people might ask: Do we actually need to create more organizations? Should we not support the ones that already exist? To them, I suggest that there remains a lot of room in the philanthropic spectrum, with most of it at the very small and very local end of the pool.

I am a huge fan of community foundations. They are incredible assets to any community, and the best of them are visionary exemplars of leadership that invest in communities in ways that business, government and the financial markets often cannot. People rightfully love their community foundations. But most people don't think the community foundation is for them. Most people believe that community foundations are where rich, old, mostly white people leave their money. They don't relate to their community foundation because they don't have a $1,000,000, $100,000 or even $10,000 to give. Even if they do, they may be years away from such philanthropic largesse; they see themselves as either too poor or too young to give at this time. Smart community foundations have begun to try to change this stereotypical perception, but it is tough to do.

The Cleveland Foundation took up the mantle of economic development over a decade ago. They have funded many kinds of unconventional projects. One their most daring was a seven-year experiment called the Civic Innovation Lab. From 2003 to 2010, the Lab provided $30,000 grants to launch upcoming entrepreneurs, then matched grant recipients with successful mentors in the regional business community.

The Lab was intended to cultivate an entrepreneurial culture in the Greater Cleveland area, which it certainly did. Over the life of the program, the economic impact of the $2.3 million invested by the Foundation was estimated at $20 million; several hundred jobs were created as well[i] This unconventional investment changed the way people viewed the Cleveland Foundation. The organization became relevant to a whole host of new people when it became a direct supporter of the business community. Philanthropy now meant business investment as well as the traditional notions of giving. People who had not been big supporters of the community foundation—in this case, the business and entrepreneurial community of Cleveland—now saw that the foundation was supporting their interests.

An even more direct example comes from the Community Foundation of Greater Muskegon in Western Michigan. After I led a community engagement workshop there and the Community Foundation saw how popular the idea of a $500 micro-grant was with attendees, the Foundation decided to open up a whole new line of grants. Their $500 Community Improvement grant has a simple, one-page application and is designed to channel such micro-funds into the hands of people who would likely not qualify for grants from other sources. The Community Foundation simplified the process and made it approachable for everyday citizens. Those who apply for the micro grants now see the Foundation as more relevant and engaged with the community at a grassroots level. Potential funders see that grants as small as $500 are part of the foundation's reach into the community. You and I may not have tens of thousands of dollars to donate to our local community foundation, but if we see that something as small as $500 is impactful, we can envision ourselves as investors who might benefit the foundation and our community.

Professional fundraisers, philanthropic organizations, faith-based groups and even Salvation Army bell ringers know a simple truth; giving is a habit. It is a habit that needs to start young—well before one becomes "rich." Younger philanthropists will someday grow into the major investors that community foundations typically target. But long before they show up on the traditional community foundation's radar, these potential donors may find new and different avenues for their version of philanthropy, outlets more in line with their values and interests.

In the summer of 2009, three young professionals from Boston, Tim Hwang, Emily Daniels and Jon Pierce, came up with a new twist on the traditional giving circle. They created the Awesome Foundation (awesomefoundation.org), a group of ten friends who donated $100 each month to provide a monthly grant of $1000 to projects they collectively decided were "awesome." The goal was to fund fun, weird, wacky projects that would likely not qualify for support from traditional sources. The guidelines were entirely self-imposed and completely flexible. They group did not form a legal entity; they were just friends who wanted to put their money back into their community. Their first grant funded the creation of a giant hammock that seats up to forty people. Why? Because it was awesome! This type of project would not have found a home with the arts council; not enough artistic content. Nor would it have flown with the community foundation; "where is the social good?" But it found its niche with a small group of citizens who wanted to do something different and fun for their community.

Since then, more than sixty Awesome Foundation chapters have formed all over the world. I have been personally active in two, Tampa Bay and St. Petersburg, and feel a bit of responsibility for the existence of a chapter in Whangarei, New Zealand, where I shared the idea with some local co-creators and they ran with it.

For those who want to start an Awesome Foundation or a similar giving circle, let me share couple of lessons learned in Tampa Bay and St. Petersburg. We opted to give quarterly grants, which obligated donors to less commitment in terms of time and finances. It is challenging to assemble ten busy people once a quarter, let alone once a month. We also learned that you have to really work to get prospective applicants to think differently about the nature of Awesome grants. Because we have come to expect, as a culture, that grants have to benefit important, noble or altruistic goals, initial submissions to the Awesome Tampa Bay and St. Petersburg Foundations were a bit more serious than we expected. The first grant we gave away was for a community food bank to purchase a used industrial refrigerator. A fine project but not necessarily fun, whimsical or likely to inspire someone to say, "That's awesome!" We learned that you have to show some crazy examples of what you hope to inspire in your community in order to elicit like-minded proposals. Still, we have been very satisfied with the results and the community response. The best part is that unlike a more formal organization, you and your nine friends get to make the rules, which again, is awesome!

Most people don't think they can be philanthropists. They think of philanthropy as something rich, old people do. Even if they are doing well financially, most people don't think they have the large amounts of money and time necessary to be philanthropic.

There will be time for that later in their lives and careers, they think. I have heard from several different community foundations about the future of philanthropy, and they are scrambling. The next generation does not give in the same way that current and past generations have. They are less attached to traditional institutions and very comfortable with the idea of circumventing such agencies via new alternatives like Kickstarter and the Awesome Foundation. We may love the United Way or the Susan G. Komen Foundation, but when we give our dollars to those organizations, we don't see the impact in the same way that we do in a micro-funded, hyper-local project. Next generation philanthropists are cutting their teeth on socially-driven, hyper-local projects that they feel like they are shaping first-hand. Foundations and charitable organizations would do well to take note, because future philanthropists will be far less likely to stroke a check and be done with it. They will want to see where their money is being allocated, they will have passions and pet projects they want funded, and they will want to be more hands-on and involved throughout the process. This shift in expectations necessitates some change on the part of our existing philanthropic organizations.

Cities and philanthropic organizations everywhere need to meet these emerging supporters where they live and start having a conversation about giving much, much earlier. Cities and philanthropic organizations need to create programs that appeal to rising donors such as micro-grants, direct interaction with grantees and ways to donate non-monetary resources. Doing so will encourage more involvement and grow the philanthropic culture in your community. People who would never have thought of themselves as philanthropists will see how easy and impactful giving even a few hundred dollars can be. They will see themselves as funders and by extension, city builders.

AIM LOW

When asked for their input, citizens are generally eager to provide all kinds of ideas and suggestions for ways a city can improve. Most of their wish list tends to consist of big changes like better schools, roads, light rail, funding for the arts and affordable housing. All of these are worthy goals but not projects citizens can directly effectuate. When citizens make such suggestions, they expect to hand them off to the city and say go make this happen. Adding more work to an already thinly stretched city staff is not a happy outcome, which explains why so many city leaders dread community input meetings. Similarly, when we ask citizens about projects that they might want to see happen, they often cite big, long-term projects. Again, I applaud the vision of citizens and the desire to better their city. The problem with big projects is that they require big budgets, lots of time and constant management. Big projects will likely discourage citizens because they require so many incremental steps—think about how many people and departments have to sign off on any project that requires new construction. Think of the insurance and permits necessary, not to mention the financial resources required, and you can see why the process infuriates people. City making, especially big city making, is a tough job that requires lots of time, money and expertise. That is why I advise citizens and even official city leaders to do something that seems contrary to their aspirations: I advise them to aim low.

By aiming low, I mean to take on simple, easy-to-execute projects that do not require big budgets and multiple players. If you can avoid the lawyers and the insurance guys, your life will be much happier. Start with lightweight, fast and inexpensive projects to get started. Gain confidence and experience by completing something simple and build from there. It would be great to have a home run in your first at bat, but in reality you would just like to get on base and maybe score a run.

We must also teach citizens how to aim low. The common notion of city building is that it involves large projects and big budgets. So when people start thinking about projects, they pitch at a high, mostly inappropriate level. They also don't see the value and impact of smaller projects. We need to change people's orientation to projects and the nature of city building.

THE $500 PROJECT

 As part of the community workshops I have been leading over the past several years, we do an exercise that has proven to be a hit with participants. I call it the "$500 Project." I show lots of examples of fun, cheap and creative projects led by citizens all over the country, then I challenge participants with this question: If you had $500 to make your city a better, more interesting, more lovable place, what would you do? This exercise works because it pitches at the right level. If I had said $10,000, or even $5,000, that is too much money. While $5,000 is a rounding error on many city project budgets, it seems like real money to most citizens. It makes them think that they need committees to manage the project. But $500 pitches at a level where you could look around the table and raise $500 from what people have in their wallets. It signifies a project that we could do next weekend with some supplies from Home Depot. It opens up the possibility for citizens to see themselves as the doers, not the city. This is the key shift. People have to believe that they can make things happen, and they need to see that small, hyper-local projects can have big impact. Once they learn this lesson, they will begin to see opportunities everywhere and, hopefully, they will become the grassroots, bottom-up complement to the city's top-down, big project efforts.

Cities for the most part get the big stuff right. There is a playbook for city making at the city scale, and all kinds of best practices and consultants to help cities through major projects. But there is no playbook for small, quirky, citizen-led endeavors. Show me the page on river monsters in the city manager's handbook! Maybe after the success of the Muscatine River Monster (described in Chapter Two) there might be one, but the handbook can't keep up with the creativity and innovation of citizen co-creators. Their creativity and unpredictability are the keys to their value in communities. Co-creators and the projects they initiate are the magic variable—the unexpected X-factor—critical to making great places. If we all follow the handbook, the established formulas, we all arrive at about the same results. When we add the co-creative variable to the mix, we get the extra spice of something different and the possibility of something amazing.

WHERE'S THE FUN? EMBRACE THE SILLY, NONSEN-SICAL AND THE WEIRD.

City building, management and governance is important work, but it does not have to be humorless. I attribute our assumption that it does to one of the better aspects of human nature. It seems that when we are tasked with doing something for our cities to serve the public good, we rise to the occasion and treat that trust with diligence and respect. We take it very seriously. But in doing so, we have lost sight of the need for, and importance of, fun. Our leaders don't want to make mistakes, but they are also deathly afraid of being seen as a lightweight, silly, frivolous or immature. So they go too far in the other direction and in doing so eliminate the fun, the play and the joy that can be found in our communities.

I challenge groups all the time with the question "Where's the fun?" We have all been in horrible, energy-draining meetings where we wrestle with the technical problems of our city, our business or organization. Those meetings suck. To that end, I challenge people, the next time they are in such a meeting, to raise a hand and ask the question "Where's the fun?" Because by asking that question, you can change the dynamic in the room and reframe the way people are looking at a problem. If you are down in the weeds, wrestling with a technical problem, then you are most likely to get a technically sufficient solution. But if you ask "Where's the fun?" you open up people's minds to the possibility of something beyond a merely technical solution that may transcend the problem at hand and provide something beyond the minimum requirements.

In Montgomery, Alabama, I spoke with the head of the city's parks and recreation department, who shared a story with me. He recalled that about a year and a half earlier, a young man and his girlfriend came into the parks and recreation office seeking a permit for an outdoor event. The couple were not your typical Montgomery residents; they were "Goths" with dark clothing, tattoos and eyeliner. And they did not want to do a typical outdoor event. They wanted to stage Montgomery's first ever zombie walk. The city official laughed as he recounted the story, admitting that he had no idea what a zombie walk was. After listening to their description, he told the couple that they would be the only two people at the event. Nonetheless he approved the request, wished them good luck and assumed he would never hear from them again. A few months later, the official recounted, he was amazed to see over 400 zombies parading through downtown

Montgomery. He was even more surprised the following year, when the event attracted twice as many participants.

Rob Bliss from Grand Rapids, Michigan, was a young professional working in social media for a local television station. He would later became nationally recognized for producing the amazing "Grand Rapids Lip Dub," the viral video sensation that was his city's response to being declared a "dying city" by Newsweek magazine in 2011.[ii] Long before Bliss produced the Grand Rapids Lip Dub, he organized some very silly, nonsensical projects. In 2008, he held a community pillow fight in one of the city's parks. In 2010, he installed a giant waterslide in the heart of downtown. Silly? Yes. Fun? Absolutely. But imagine if some city official had said to him, "We are not that kind of city." They not only would have missed out on those fun projects, they would probably have not gotten the Grand Rapids Lip Dub. Part of Rob's success was that he built on a series of smaller projects to the point where he could pull off the comparatively massive Lip Dub effort. More importantly, he was not squelched by his city along the way. If someone had told him "no" I suspect Bliss would have been far less inclined to step up for his community when it actually needed him.

Silly, weird and frivolous projects can be very important. They are the proving ground for community activists and co-creators. This is where such co-creators get their feet wet and gain experience that can later be applied to larger and perhaps more significant projects. Playful projects also send a message to your community about what you value: tolerance and fun. If the community accepts weird and wacky projects, they are probably good with weird and wacky people. They are going to be welcoming of diversity of color, creed, sexual orientation and ideas. And they are showing that they are a fun community. A community the says "yes" to unusual projects is likely a community that says "yes" to its young people and has room for something beyond standard issue, conventional notions of fun.

In advocating for such projects, I am fully aware that some, most in fact, may not be winners. Trying to pick the winners is like trying to pick a winning stock. The best solution is to diversify. City leadership understandably finds it difficult to initiate the weird, wacky and different. It is not in their nature, and that is fine. Cities need an engaged citizenry, with their different ways of thinking and their freedom from political strictures, to provide the fun, the X-factor in making vibrant places. Squelch the enthusiasm, enforce the rules to the point of being no fun, or be so difficult to work with that people would rather circumvent you or just not even bother at all, and you have effectively removed the creativity and imagination of your citizens from the game.

A SPECIAL THOUGHT FOR CITIES AND CITY LEADERSHIP: HAVE A SENSE OF HUMOR, ESPECIALLY ABOUT YOURSELF.

Cities need to have a sense of humor. Sometimes it even needs to be about themselves. Fort Wayne, Indiana, had a unique opportunity to laugh at itself and sadly opted on the side of caution and chose to not show a sense of humor. In 2011, the city was seeking to name its new downtown municipal building. In an effort to be inclusive, they sought community input and even ran an online poll.

The overwhelming favorite (receiving over 80 percent of 30,000 votes cast) was to name the building after a beloved former mayor of Fort Wayne named Harry Baals. Baals was Fort Wayne's mayor from 1934-1947 and again from 1951-1954. Yes, he pronounced his name "balls." His descendants changed the pronunciation to "bales," but that did not matter.

The community voted, and they wanted the new building to be called the Harry Baals Government Center. I laugh even as I write it, and that is O.K. In fact it is better than O.K.—it is memorable, funny and a little bawdy. Using the name would have shown that the city had a sense of humor, a sense of history and enough confidence that it could take a joke in stride. But city officials didn't make that choice. Fearing ridicule, they opted to call the new building Citizens Square, despite the informal popular vote. National media picked up the story, and everyone from Rush Limbaugh to Jimmy Kimmel made fun of the city. At the building's grand opening, Fort Wayne's mayor explained that the city had decided it didn't want to name the building after any single person.[iii] If that sounds hollow to you, join the club. Fort Wayne could have shined had they proudly said, the people have spoken and we will honor the city's longest serving mayor by naming our municipal building after him. Instead, they looked a bit weak, embarrassed and utterly lacking a sense of humor.

ENGAGE YOUR FAITH-BASED COMMUNITY

In July 2013, I had the opportunity to speak to the very progressive United Church of Christ at their biannual General Synod. This is a national congress that brings together thousands of people and hundreds of church leaders from around the country. The group had asked me to speak on the issue of community engagement. Over the previous two years, I had spoken with a couple of faith-based groups but never to one so large and as important as UCC. Prior keynote speakers included PBS commentator Bill Moyers, Children's Defense Fund president Marian Wright Edelman and then-senator Barack Obama, so I was feeling some pressure to find the right message for this influential group.

As I thought about the role that faith-based groups play in community development, one key point I kept coming back to was their amazing capacity to marshal volunteers for a variety of efforts, from bake sales to a neighborhood cleanups. Churches are central organizers of our desire to connect and give back to our communities. For many people, the church provides a "gateway" for their desire to give something back, be it money, time or other resources. The church helps to channel their desire into action. The significance of this role of entry point cannot be underestimated. There are many people who would like to become more engaged in their communities, but they have no idea where to begin. They don't know where to spend their time or resources, and they don't necessarily know who or what is "real" and worthy of investment. The church provides the trusted vehicle that they can use to get in the game.

For many, becoming active church members who regularly volunteer will satisfy their urge to give. But a small percentage will choose to conceive and develop their own projects, perhaps a passion project or life's calling that would not have been realized without the experience and confidence gained by volunteering through their faith-based organization. We don't think of such organizations as training grounds for city building, but they absolutely serve that role as one of the many benefits that they confer upon their communities.

Church leadership might consider encouraging their most activist members to imagine new projects, perhaps even ones that extend beyond the physical boundaries of the church, to contribute to the city. City leadership would do well to note the ranks of church activists and engage with them. These co-creators most likely only need a cause or a challenge from their city to shift their efforts into the broader community realm.

BREAK SOME RULES

Sometimes you have to break a few rules in order to move the needle and change the dialogue. A great example of this occurred in January 2012 when Matt Tomasulo of Raleigh, North Carolina, decided to post some signs in the heart of downtown Raleigh. The signs, geared towards people, not cars, displayed the walking distance to various Raleigh landmarks, such as "It's a 5 minute walk to city center."

Photo courtesy dtraleigh / walkyourcity.org

Tomasulo, a graduate student in city planning, created the signs as part of his master's project. His premise was simple enough: to encourage more walking by "just offering the idea that it's O.K. to walk... People just don't even think about walking as a choice right now," said Tomasulo.[iv]

The signs looked official and they weren't advertising, so many people, including police officers and even some city staff, assumed they were authorized by the city. About a month after the signs had been posted, city officials realized what was going on and took the signs down. A flurry of negative press followed; it turned out that Raleigh residents loved the signs and felt like the city was squelching something cool by removing them. Raleigh Planning Director Mitchell Silver was a fan of the signs and looked for ways to get them back up. "I've never seen this level of civic participation from this generation since the 1960s, when I grew up," said Silver, who is also president of the American Planning Association. "I wanted to endorse that level of creativity and innovation."[v]

Supporters gathered more than 1,200 signatures in support of the signs in just three days and used this leverage to cajole the city council into authorizing a "pilot program" that brought back the signs, to the delight of locals. Since then, the project has spawned an organization, Walk Your City (walkyourcity. org), and has spread to over twenty other cities.

Tomasulo's project is a great example of how sometimes you need to break the rules to introduce constructive change. As much as Mitchell Silver loved the idea of the signs, his planning office was not the entity that would have gone out and posted the signs without official approval. He was not in a position to be a rule-breaker, but he clearly saw the opportunity to facilitate change once it arrived.

I am a lawyer by training. One of the things that I remember well from law school is the adage about the letter of the law and the spirit of the law. Much of jurisprudence is about the tension that exists between these two poles and how such tension actually causes the law to evolve. This is a good thing, and it makes for a living legal system. In our cities, there are the rules (city codes, forms, requirements, policies and procedures) and there is the goal: a better, more interesting, more lovable city.

Sometimes the rules don't allow us to attain the goal in the most expeditious manner, or even to get there at all. That is inherently frustrating to the typical citizen, who sees Byzantine rule systems as an impediment rather than a social framework. Truth be told, rules can be both. It is very difficult for those who have written the rules and are tasked with enforcing them to go out and break those rules, even in the name of a better, more interesting or more lovable city. I often see elected officials and city staff chomp at the bit to do the guerrilla projects that I tell them about in conversations and presentations. But they can't because they are the establishment, and they recognize that it can be seen as a breach of the public trust if they are too proactive in skirting the rules. If the mayor or a city council member is breaking this or that little rule, even with the best of intentions, there are those (particularly in our scandal-obsessed media) who would jump to the conclusion that the same individual may be breaking other rules and regulations. Best to leave the rule breaking to those who can afford, politically, to take more risks.

Those who can take risks need the support of those who can't. If you can't expose yourself or your office to potential backlash, you need to find ways to encourage and even protect those who do take those risks. Have their backs.

HOW TO GET AWAY WITH IT

I was recently asked during a Q&A session how to get away with the rule breaking that I often argue is necessary to advance our cities. I jokingly replied, "Be faster and sneakier than those who would thwart you." Based on my experience, there's something to this advice, though I originally offered it as somewhat tongue-in-cheek. And it's not really that high of a bar to clear. Your intentions will make a huge difference. Projects like Walk Raleigh and Swings Tampa Bay had no overt advertising or commercial connection, which made a significant difference in how they were perceived. A for-profit venture, no matter how cool, is likely to generate scrutiny. So if you break rules, come at it from an altruistic place. If caught, your best defense is the fact that you were trying to do something positive for your community and not trying to make a buck.

BE BOLD

In Edmonton, Canada, a movement called "I 'Heart' YEGDT" started in 2012. YEG is the airport code for Edmonton, and DT stands for downtown. A local blogger made up his own t-shirt with the "I 'Heart' YEGDT" message on it and wore it while performing at the city's Pecha Kucha Night. The audience loved it, and downtown merchants, residents and fans took the idea and expanded it.

One of the campaign's first public manifestations was the appearance of dozens of spray painted logos on sidewalks and walls throughout downtown. I met two of the guys who spray-painted the "I 'Heart' YEGDT" stencils all over downtown. They laughed when I asked them how they got away with it. They said it was easy; they just got a couple of orange safety vests, put on hard hats and acted like they were told to do it. To quote Ferris Bueller: "The meek get pinched. The bold survive."

Once the logo and idea was out there, t-shirts and other print products quickly followed. Local restaurants encouraged their wait staff to wear the t-shirts and buttons. Signs appeared in windows all throughout the downtown retail community. Local construction companies even got on board and added the logo to their temporary walls in the downtown core.

Sometimes it takes a good idea and a couple of risk-takers to set things in motion. Other times, it takes people who are willing to question the rules. Reuben Pressman, my friend from Swings Tampa Bay, observes that, "the rules don't always tell you what's right. Rules change all the time." So remember, if you can't be a risk-taker, support those who do take the risk.

BE EMOTIONALLY TRUE

Cities, be they big or small, exhibit a familiar pattern when talking about themselves. Our chambers of commerce, tourist boards, mayors and economic development departments are all trying to cast their community in the best light. Marketing 101 tells us to differentiate ourselves from our competitors. Brand strategists encourage us to create a memorable identity. Site selection specialists advise us to promote our economic advantages. All of this advice is perfectly valid, but far too often such messages feel like they are lacking something. I used to think what they were lacking was "authenticity"—a buzzword that is bandied about communities to champion the local, different and unique aspects of those places. Turns out what is most often missing is even more fundamental. Most messaging lacks heart and emotional truth. I learned this lesson in Garland, Texas.

Garland is one of the cities that ring the Dallas-Fort Worth metro area and would in most cases be called a satellite city. But like most things in Texas, Garland (population 226,000) is too large to be thought of simply as a satellite. Garland residents do, however, have to work hard to escape the long shadow cast by Dallas and Fort Worth. Interestingly, Garland has the distinction of being the cowboy hat capital of Texas. [vi] The city is home to four of the nation's largest cowboy hat manufacturers, including Resistol, Hatco and Milano, which make the brands Stetson and Wrangler. Garland produces more than a million cowboy hats each year and can rightly call itself the cowboy hat capital of Texas. I met with Garland Mayor

Douglas Athas and, as we talked, I mentioned that the cowboy hat claim was a notable distinction for Garland. He smiled and said something that I thought was brilliant; he said the cowboy hat capital distinction was "factually true but not emotionally true." He told me to look around as we walked through Firewheel Town Center. No one was wearing a cowboy hat. Yes, Garland produces more cowboy hats than any other U.S. city, but to the average Garland resident, that fact did not reflect day-to-day reality. It was not emotionally true to the people of Garland. Being to the east of Dallas, Garland did not have the same cowboy culture that exists in Fort Worth. This was a point I did understand. I had been to the region before and knew that Fort Worth, to the west of Dallas, has a much more overt cowboy culture than other cities in the region. Dallas is a global business city, but Fort Worth was once described to me as "a city of Texans."

Mayor Athas said that Garland needed to find something that was emotionally true to distinguish itself from other places. The answer was not too far from the hat manufacturing identity. Garland is home to over 350 other advanced manufacturing firms as well. Thus they selected as their identity, "Texas Made Here," which is not only factually true, as the city's manufacturing sector employs thousands, but far more emotionally true to the community as a whole.

Emotional truth matters, and I had not reflected on it until Mayor Athas planted the seed. Cities everywhere spend millions on branding and identity in the hope of creating a vision for citizens as well as luring tourists and businesses to their community. Such campaigns work best when they feel real to us. The cowboy hat idea did not feel real to the majority of folks in Garland, but "Texas Made Here" rang true as an identity. If your branding does not match the emotional truth of your place, then you have a problem.

Gonzales, California, is in the heart of northern California's agricultural center, also known as the "salad bowl" of Monterey County. Gonzales (population 8,187) makes the claim of being the "Wine Capital of Monterey County" because it is the home of a large wine production facility owned by Constellation Brands. Constellation Brands is a huge beverage company, and they tout themselves as the "#1 premium wine producer in the world,"[vii] as well as the "#1 multi-category beverage alcohol company in the U.S."[viii] In contrast to these distinctions, the company's presence in Gonzales does not take the form of an archetypal vineyard. Rather, Constellation occupies a large factory that is outwardly indistinguishable from any other industrial facility. I was in Gonzales during what the community calls "The Crush," when millions of pounds of grapes are literally crushed to begin the wine-making process. You could smell the grapes in the air, and that was certainly memorable. However, The Crush only happens a couple times each year. The plant includes a tasting room, but it is not generally open to the public and is only used for special occasions.

I understand that you can make the technical argument that Gonzales is the wine capital of the region based on Constellation's significant presence, but this city to me did not feel like a "wine capital." In talking with people from Gonzales, I also did not get the impression that they had a strong connection to the city's identity as a wine capital. They were far more invested in their advanced agricultural businesses and their central position in the agricultural identity of the region. If the locals don't buy into and believe in the stated identity, it is very hard to get others to in believe it.

This is not to say that you can't "fake it 'til you make it," but eventually you have to pay off the promise and become what you have declared yourself to be in a way that does ring true emotionally. This is exactly what happened in St. Petersburg, Florida.

In 2009, the St. Petersburg Downtown Arts Association, a non-profit coalition of the city's galleries and arts institutions declared St. Petersburg to be a "City of the Arts" based on the large number of arts organizations in the city. It was clearly an aspirational goal. "City of the Arts" is a lofty designation, one we would more likely associate with New York, Paris or Florence. The Southeast does not have the arts and cultural tradition of other regions in the U.S. My artist friends rolled their eyes at the statement and asked how we could be a city of the arts but not be supportive of actual artists. This was a valid question and indicative of the lack of emotional truth in the statement at the time. Nonetheless, several key things happened to change the situation. The Craftsman House Gallery championed a campaign in the magazine *American Style* to get St. Pete designated an arts destination by including materials on how to vote for the city in all of their patrons' bags. The tactic worked, and St. Pete was named a Top 25 Arts Destination by the magazine in 2009.[ix] The city took note of this success and in 2010 developed a cultural marketing plan and an economic impact study, which led to being declared the #1 mid-sized arts destination by American Style for three straight years.[x] I find it fascinating and amusing that the plan followed the Top 25 designation, and not the other way around!

The emotional truth of St. Petersburg's being a city of the arts came about in a six-month period, from July 2010 to January 2011. In July 2010, the Chihuly Collection opened in the city's downtown. This permanent exhibition of the hugely popular glass artist Dale Chihuly's work was, at the time, the only museum dedicated to his art outside of his home city, Seattle. Six months later, in January 2011, a newly rebuilt Salvador Dalí Museum opened at the southern end of the downtown waterfront. The prior Dalí Museum had been located several blocks south of downtown and was not within walking distance for most residents. Moreover, the original museum was actually a converted warehouse. Despite this, the museum had been a huge cultural draw for the city and a true gem for the region, but its location did not allow much synergy between it and the rest of downtown. The new museum building, with its bold architectural design, was located on the waterfront and within easy walking distance of downtown and other cultural assets including the Museum of Fine Arts, St. Petersburg, and the Chihuly Collection.

Arts and cultural advocates and artists will take issue with my contention that a museum makes a city a cultural destination. They will note (correctly) that arts and culture is about the creative people and organizations making art. Museums are essentially boxes that we fill with content, and the content is the art, not the edifice. True. But to most people, the building is a visible and persistent reminder of art and culture. Even if they never go inside the museum, they see its exterior, and it creates an impression. The opening of two notable museums, especially the Dalí, in downtown St. Petersburg made the case in the hearts and minds of locals that the city was truly a city of the arts. We faked it for a while, but we found ways to make the identity real. We started small, built on momentum and were fortunate enough to cap things off with the opening of a dramatic anchor institution.

Emotional truth feels different from technical truth or marketing spin. We all have pretty good emotional radars, and cities should not underestimate our capacity to know what is real and what is B.S. It is time for some self-reflection and honesty. Look at your own marketing and messaging and ask if there is emotional truth to match whatever clever branding you are promoting. Look deeper into your community and let emotional truth be a litmus test for the work you do. When something is emotionally true for your community, you will know it. More importantly, your community will know it, too.

Chapter Two
Try This

Once we buy into the idea that love and emotional engagement with our places matter, the next question is: How do we do it? This is a fair question. Unlike most other aspects of our cities, there is no playbook for emotional engagement. There are no established "best practices" that cities can emulate in their efforts to become more lovable and engaging places. You can't decree love. You can't buy love. You can, however, create a set of conditions where love might happen—"might" being the operative word. "Might" is not a word that civic leaders tend to embrace. It is too vague and fuzzy by commonly held standards. Such leaders make promises based on deliverable goals, and we hold them accountable for their pronouncements. Announcing that a road *might* be built or that the police *might* show up when called is not how leaders get re-elected. But in the arena of emotions, there are no guarantees. If we are going to engage the emotional side of our cities, we need to be O.K. with misses. Not everyone we date is going to love us, but we still need to put ourselves out there. We experiment in the emotional realm until we get it right and find the person we truly love.

Communities will need to "date" and to experiment to find out what clicks. Included here are some practices that might work for you. These examples might spark an idea or a movement that becomes a big victory for your city—or they might fizzle. Either way, we can learn something along the way, and if we remain committed to the process we will get better at it.

EVERY COMMUNITY NEEDS MORE LOVE NOTES

In *For the Love of Cities*, I introduced the idea of "love notes," those comparatively small projects, actions and interventions that have outsized impact on the way people feel about their community. The love note metaphor was based on the significance that a hand-written note has on the way we feel about the gift it accompanies and, by extension, the person giving it. Though small, such a gesture has an outsized impact on the way we feel. The idea of the love note in cities was a natural fit. I had experienced the effect myself as I had traveled and observed amazing examples of small things that citizens loved about their communities—features that were disproportionate to their importance in the scheme of traditional economic development accounting. Such token urban characteristics (e.g., events, monuments, neighborhood quirks) are often overlooked or seen as non-essential, even frivolous, in tough economic times. These love notes, even the most temporary, have proven time and again to have immense value to their communities. They are emotional anchors for our perceptions and memories of places. To illustrate what I mean, here are some of my favorite love notes—ones I have found since writing *For the Love of Cities*—from cities around the U.S.

SWINGS TAMPA BAY, ST. PETERSBURG, FLORIDA

In November 2010, a swing appeared on the campus of the University of South Florida in St. Petersburg. It was hand-painted and suspended from a tree on campus, and it was twice as wide as an ordinary swing so that two people could sit side-by-side on it. The swing was the work of Hunter Payne, then an art student at the university, and its appearance stemmed from his participation in an environmental design class. His assignment was to alter the campus in some way, so Hunter decided to hang a swing. His reasoning was that the swing would be a community-building exercise. People would see the swing, sit in it, laugh and interact with each other. His idea was remarkably simple, but it didn't stop there. Along with his best friend, Reuben Pressman, he started Swings Tampa Bay and began to hang swings all over the Tampa Bay area. The two young men organized painting parties to decorate the wooden swings with art and encouraged others to go out and hang the swings, which they gave away. And people took them up on their offer. Over 250 swings were hung throughout the community. Some remained in place for weeks while others, such as one they installed on a pedestrian bridge over the local interstate, lasted only a few hours before city workers took it down.

I asked Hunter and Reuben about their goals for this seemingly silly project. They said they hoped that the swings would help people change their daily routines, spark new curiosity about their everyday environment and show other St. Pete residents that something different was possible. They also shared with me how the various cities that comprise Tampa Bay responded to the swings. Some authorities told Hunter and Rueben that, officially, they were obligated to take the swings down—but, unofficially, many law enforcement officers liked the project and its goals. That positive feedback, Hunter and Reuben told me, had been a wonderful surprise. It shows that cities are not always the draconian enforcers of rules that we believe them to be. The reality is that, at least in the context of Swings Tampa Bay, some individuals in city government have a sense of perspective and welcome the prospect of fun. This is promising. There are risk takers in our bureaucracies. We need to encourage such individuals to find a balance between rules and the goal of nurturing a better, more interesting and more lovable city. This is not an easy thing to do, and we should have sympathy for those daring bureaucrats. They inhabit a professional environment where they are encouraged to say "no." I even have heard some describe how their colleagues use creativity to find new and different ways to deny requests. Changing that kind of culture is difficult, but I know risk takers exist in every city government. We just need to keep coming up with new, novel, fun and beneficial love notes so that even the crustiest of bureaucrats will find it hard to say no!

MICE ON MAIN, GREENVILLE, SOUTH CAROLINA

Greenville, South Carolina, claims to have the best downtown in the U.S., and they make a pretty strong case for it. Greenville's Main Street runs for several blocks with an incredible tree canopy, dozens of local shops and restaurants that culminate in the fantastic Falls Park. The park, located at the west end of downtown, features a gorgeous 100-meter long pedestrian bridge spanning the waterfall of the Reedy River. Falls Park is all the more remarkable because an auto bridge covered it for decades. Over twenty years ago, some Greenville citizens had the audacious idea of closing the bridge to cars and making it into a pedestrian-only zone. Many folks thought it idiotic to tear down a perfectly good bridge in favor of a park and feared a loss of commercial traffic. (Similar arguments were heard when New York City proposed to make Times Square into a pedestrian-only zone in 2009). After much debate, renovation on Falls Park began in the 1990s, and the pedestrian bridge opened in 2004. People marveled at how beautiful the bridge and the river were, and the park became downtown's primary destination. Now Greenville is seen as a textbook example of downtown revitalization success that other cities seek to emulate.

I visited Greenville in the summer of 2013 and was very impressed with the downtown. Yet amidst the city's great urbanism, the aspect of downtown I remember most—the one that truly made me smile—was the "Mice on Main." This little project was created by a high school student named Jim Ryan. Ryan approached Greenville mayor Knox White in 2000 with the idea of creating nine tiny bronze mice that would be placed in the downtown core on Main Street. The idea was to make a scavenger hunt that would allow people to explore the city on foot. The mayor loved the idea and the price tag: under $2000. Today, if you visit downtown Greenville, you will see people walking the downtown with special maps in hand as they search for the mice. Visitors laugh and exclaim with delight when they find one, and taking a photograph is a typical reaction. Each of the mice has a name, all starting with the letter "M," and each has a personal history. There is even a children's book called *The Mice on Main* that chronicles their adventures.

Photo by Peter Kageyama

Surprise and delight go a long way towards making cities memorable and lovable. The moment of discovering one of Greenville's bronze mice, and then laughing at the charm of the idea, is priceless. Generating fun, surprise and delight do not have to cost a lot of money, but they do require us to think of those emotions as legitimate and expected goals of the urban revitalization projects we undertake. When did you last see fun, surprise or delight openly articulated as a goal of an economic development project? Most likely never—and that is a missed opportunity. If we put fun on our list of serious goals, we challenge those associated with the work of city development to at least be thinking about the possibilities. And if they are thinking of fun as a supplementary goal, they may come up with something wonderful that potentially increases the overall value and experience of the core project. It may not always be a home run, but even a moment of surprise and delight can have lasting value.

I SEE WHAT YOU MEAN, DENVER, COLORADO

As part of the 2004 renovation of its convention center, the City of Denver was looking for a signature piece of public art that would highlight the new building. They selected regional artist Lawrence Argent, who proposed to make a 40-foot tall statue of a bear peering into the windows of the convention center. The color of the bear was to be blue. Can you imagine the many conversations this proposal must have sparked? Many people are already skeptical of public art, so a giant blue bear would just provide even more ammunition to attack the project. Argent said his concept came from newspaper stories about curious bears coming into the city during a recent drought. The image of the curious bear stuck with him, and when it came time to conceive of a project for the convention center Argent's idea was that local Coloradans, like the curious bear, were eager to know about what went on inside the convention center and would want to peek inside. Despite some initial community reticence, when the statue—titled *I See What You Mean*—debuted in 2005, people immediately "got it." Some things have to be seen and experienced to be fully appreciated. The sculpture created a buzz and a must-see photo opportunity for downtown Denver. "Beloved" is now a term often used for the bear, and it has become an icon of the city. It is also a fantastic love note for Denver and all who visit its convention center.

The big blue bear should remind cities everywhere not only about the importance of public art but also about the importance of surprise and delight. If you were to look at the pure economic cost and benefits of the big blue bear, you could not justify it. Think of how many potholes you could fix for the amount of money the sculpture cost to build. So if city building is just about the bottom line, you will never do anything like the big blue bear. You will never do anything fun or beautiful or whimsical, because on a purely financial basis it does not make sense. But we do irrational things like adorning a convention center with a giant, curious bear because we recognize that surprise and delight have value. Kudos to Denver for not doing "safe" public art, either. The city did something different and playful, which made it vulnerable to accusations of being silly and frivolous— something no official wants to be tagged with. By taking a bit of a risk, Denver's officials created something special and very valuable.

The value of the bear sculpture is that once you see Denver's big blue bear, you will never forget it. The first time you see the sculpture you cannot help but smile, laugh and (of course) take a picture. There is value in those smiles and good will. The experience becomes an anchor for your memories of Denver, and you cannot help but feel good. And look at the many photos that people have taken of the bear and spread all over the world via social media. Every one of those photos is a postcard for Denver. Think of the value of that!

FROM OFF RAMPS TO PUBLIC SPACES, CREVE COEUR, MISSOURI

Creve Coeur is an affluent suburb of St. Louis, Missouri. Located just outside the city on Interstate 270, it is best known as the location of Monsanto's global headquarters. Creve Coeur does not have a traditional downtown or city center, and that lack has been a source of consternation and discussion for the community's leadership. The city of Creve Coeur is mostly known for its many office parks, which border the freeway for easy access to commuters. During morning and evening rush hours, thousands of such commuters exit and enter the freeway at the Creve Coeur junction. It was at those junctions that town leaders found an opportunity to create a signature love note.

The on and off ramps at Creve Coeur's Olive Boulevard exit are unusually beautiful. They are extensively landscaped with public art touches, artistic signage and even some thoughtful, albeit largely underused, public green space. Some might question the expense of bringing such aesthetic attention to something as seemingly utilitarian as a freeway entrance. "It's just a freeway entrance—no one will care," would be a likely refrain. But Creve Coeur thought beyond the obvious. Recognizing that to many people, the exit and entrance ramps are their city's de facto signature, rather than a downtown, Creve Coeur made the practical decision to make this gateway as nice as possible. Such attention and effort sends a message. People will use the on and off ramps everyday. Over time, their beauty may become unremarkable to regular commuters and residents, yet on a subconscious level it continues to register that this is not your ordinary freeway exit. Such a departure from the ordinary has an effect on our emotional state. We recognize beauty and comfort even if we only pause beside it for a few minutes at the traffic light on our way home. Creve Coeur is making the best of a less than optimal situation and is doing so in a creative and cost effective way.

MUSCATINE RIVER MONSTER, MUSCATINE, IOWA

Andrew Anderson is an artist from Muscatine, Iowa, which is located on the banks of the Mississippi River. Anderson better fits the term "maker" because his art is equal parts engineering and creativity. In 2011, he wanted to promote and inspire his fellow Midwest creatives. He knew that Muscatine had a rich history of innovation, and he hoped to hit on a compelling way to tell that story. Anderson felt that he and his peers needed to do something "over the top and exciting" to tell a story "that should be really inspiring to artists and creative people."[xi] He decided to share Muscatine's narrative of innovation through the invention of a mythological creature with a history dating to 1838. In the summer of 2011, he debuted the Muscatine River Monster.

Photo by Mike Shield

The monster first appeared in the upper floors of an historic hotel in Muscatine that had recently been converted into condominiums. Anderson worked with the condominium developer to install the monster for the building's grand opening. Brilliantly, Anderson made a design decision not to show the whole monster, but instead constructed only giant pink tentacles that appeared to emerge from the building windows. Air fans caused the arms to move up and down like auto dealership inflatables, and people loved it. Extensive local and regional media coverage followed, and city residents were buzzing about the monster. Some people requested the monster for their buildings, so Anderson took the installation on the road to sites including local stores, dormitories at a community college, a public library and even the old State House in Iowa City, some forty miles away.

The Muscatine River Monster project was a way to shine a spotlight on local creativity and encourage people to pursue creative ideas, and perhaps even creative careers. In trying to inspire his community, Anderson did an amazing thing. He held up a mirror to his community and showed Muscatine residents a side of themselves they did not know was there. He showed them their creative, imaginative capacities. That is powerful. Such an action can be a game-changer for communities by altering perceptions of what is possible and what is permissible. As a result, other creative Iowans may attempt something even bigger and more adventurous than the monster, all because someone who loves their city has shown them, in dramatic fashion, that they are something more than they previously imagined.

WINTER THE DOLPHIN, CLEARWATER, FLORIDA

In December 2005, an injured young dolphin washed up on the shore of Clearwater, Florida. Caught in a fishing net that caused loss of blood flow to her tail, the young dolphin was saved by the Clearwater Marine Aquarium but had to have her tail amputated. Thus begins the heartwarming story of the dolphin named Winter. After receiving a custom prosthetic tail, Winter became a media sensation, an inspiration to people everywhere and the basis for a commercially successful Disney film, *Dolphin Tale*, released in 2011. The movie has had such an effect on local tourism that an economic impact study conducted by the University of South Florida, St. Petersburg, estimated Winter's contribution to the local economy between 2012 and 2016 to be in excess of $5 billion.[xii] Yes, that is billion with a "b."

Downtown Clearwater now boasts painted dolphin statues as part of its public art program, and images of Winter can be found everywhere. The dolphin was the centerpiece of a successful 2013 public referendum to finance a new $160 million aquarium in downtown Clearwater. Winter has become a love note for Clearwater as well as a source of huge business and an unofficial mascot for the city. No one could have imagined such an outcome back in 2005. Obviously you can't plan on having a Winter the Dolphin in your community, but if it happens— count your blessings and plan accordingly. And consider that for over five years, Winter was just a good local story and not yet a full-blown phenomenon. Your great story may already exist within your community. You just have to find it, elevate it and get a little bit lucky.

WE ARE JOPLIN, JOPLIN, MISSISSIPPI

In May 2013, I visited Joplin, Missouri. The city had been on my list of places to visit because of the terrible tornado that ripped through it in May 2011. New Orleans and Cedar Rapids, Iowa, had demonstrated that cities in recovery from the tragedy of natural disasters become incredible laboratories for civic innovation. Crisis often compels communities to take risks and embrace new ideas, and those cities become examples that other cities can emulate. In my presentations, I frequently show examples from both New Orleans and Cedar Rapids, including the amazing work of Candy Chang. Chang, an artist and community activist from New Orleans, has risen to national prominence because of her creative work and TED Talk fame. Her numerous designs include nametag stickers that read "I Wish This Was...," which Chang placed on abandoned buildings and empty storefronts after Katrina, and repurposed blackboards stenciled with the provocative phrase "Before I Die...," as a prompt for passersby to inscribe their bucket lists with pieces of chalk. The genius of these projects is that they are so simple and so accessible, yet profound in their capacity for community engagement.

Chang's projects are unusual examples of public art that invite you to interact, to become a co-creator and to play. When people share their bucket list on the "Before I Die..." wall, they are sharing hopes and dreams with fellow citizens. Such sharing is deeply personal and, when ventured, invites comments, discussion and even companionship. (You want to skydive? Me, too! Let's go this weekend.) When someone fills in the blank on a "I Wish This Was..." nametag on an empty storefront, she is essentially voting on what empty and abandoned buildings should be and proclaiming that someone cares about such spaces. When you see dozens, even hundreds, of other votes on the wall, you realize that other people care, too. The gesture says, I am not alone in this care for my community, and *that* is amazingly powerful.

As part of my talk in Joplin, I shared one of Chang's simplest projects, a stencil she made after Hurricane Katrina that read, "It's good to be here." She used spray chalk to post the message all over the city. Imagine how such a message resonated in New Orleans, a city that many people thought was lost. "It's good to be here" rang out powerfully there, and as I shared it with the folks of Joplin, it resonated with them as well.

A few weeks after I spoke in Joplin, I received an online invitation from Joplin resident Jane Cage to join an invitation-only Facebook group called "The Joplin Co-Creators Underground League." Cage, one of the main organizers of my visit, had been tremendously active in the recovery efforts in Joplin. She was even awarded a U.S. Department of Homeland Security medal for community resilience in 2012. Not surprisingly, Cage was one of the people behind a newly formed and covert group of activists who had taken my message to heart and had begun to make things happen in Joplin. They created the closed Facebook group because they wanted some anonymity and a space to discuss ideas without scrutiny because many of the members were prominent citizens within Joplin.

One of the first projects they launched was a simple riff on Candy Chang's "It's Good to Be Here" stencil. They created a "We Are Joplin" stencil and began to spray chalk the message all over the city. The statement followed the spirit of the "Restore Joplin" message that had appeared in the days following the tornado in 2011. In broad terms, such a message provides a simple reminder that a city is not something that exists only externally to us. Too often we externalize and personify cities with language: "The city should do this..." or "The city needs X." Implicit in such remarks is the notion that our city exists outside of us. By stating "We Are Joplin," the JCCUL tries to instill in people the realization that they *are* the city, and how they think and feel and act as citizens co-creates the community, at least in part. When we recognize that city making is our responsibility, as well as that of official authorities, we become co-creators and problem-solvers, not just consumers of our cities.

In the fall of 2013, many of the JCCUL members also participated in creating a downtown mural titled *I Am Joplin*, which was made up of 300 small portraits of Joplin residents printed on aluminum.[xiii] The mural, produced by Art Feeds, featured images of Joplin citizens holding messages including "I am strong," "I am hopeful" and "I am blessed," along with "I am Joplin." Again, the impact of a project like this stems from its rekindling of the connection between a city and its citizens. Through the mural, we see that Joplin is not the faceless bureaucracy that we typically think of as "the city." It is still early days for the JCCUL and the We Are Joplin movement, but looking at the Facebook group I noticed several posts by people asking when they were going to go spray chalking again.

MORE RITUALS & TRADITIONS

In *For the Love of Cities*, I highlighted the importance of community rituals and traditions. From the beauty and elegance of Waterfire in Providence to the outlandish zombie walks of Pittsburgh, such rituals have become central to community identity and create lasting emotional bonds for citizens and visitors alike. In my travels, I hear about all kinds of wonderful rituals and traditions, and I wanted to share more examples because of how powerfully they illustrate community creativity. They also illustrate community introspection. The best rituals and traditions evolve out of a community's existing identity and perceptions of itself. Its residents take that kernel of uniqueness and make it even more special by elevating and expanding it, or perhaps by turning the characteristic on its head and making us examine it and, by extension, ourselves in the process. The best of these celebratory occasions are also fun and social. Anytime you can bring people together so that they laugh and smile, you have a winning formula for your community.

BRIDGE DINNER, SHELBURNE FALLS, MASSACHU-SETTS

Shelburne Falls is a small village (population 1,731) in Franklin County in western Massachusetts. The Falls Truss Bridge, known locally as the "Iron Bridge," crosses the Deerfield River and flows through the heart of downtown. No one would ever call the Iron Bridge, which carries cars and trucks across the river, pretty. It suffers by comparison with the nearby Bridge of Flowers, a lovely pedestrian bridge that is covered by—you guessed it—flowers. But the Iron Bridge has become a beloved piece of infrastructure because every August for the past dozen years the local business association of Shelburne Falls has sponsored a bridge dinner. The association closes the bridge down to traffic, cleans it up and sets up a long dining table that seats over 400 people down the center of the bridge. Local restaurateurs cater the event, students act as wait staff and diners enjoy a lovely summer evening by having a meal together on a piece of public infrastructure.

As a local, you may pass over that bridge every day, but I guarantee that having dinner on it will make you change the way you see and think about the bridge and your city. We are locked into certain ways of viewing our world akin to "functional blindness," the failure to see beyond a single prescribed use for an object. When we see a box, we think about storage. When we see a bridge, we see transportation. But something like the bridge dinner makes you look at infrastructure with new eyes. There is beauty and fantastic engineering in even the most mundane aspects of our cities. Look at a parking garage or a sidewalk and try to appreciate all that goes into making it, and you begin to understand that we walk past such marvels everyday without much regard. Taking the time to break bread with your fellow citizens and to pause and reflect upon your city seems like a great way to spend an evening. So what might you have dinner on in your own community?

In early 2013 I visited Goleta, California, a city just outside of Santa Barbara. In my talks there, I shared the bridge dinner example, and Goleta residents loved the idea. They loved it so much that in August of the same year, they hosted their first "Dam Dinner" on the Lake Los Carneros dam. Over 250 people came out to the inaugural event to share a meal. They printed up t-shirts that read "Best Dam Dinner Ever." The t-shirts sold out in under an hour.

BLOBFEST, PHOENIXVILLE, PENNSYLVANIA

The Blob, released in 1957, is horror movie that is in most ways indistinguishable from dozens of other films that tapped into Cold War paranoia about radioactive monsters and outer space. The film most likely would have been forgotten but for its lead actor, the young Steve McQueen, who would go on to become a major movie star in 1960s and 70s. I love the film and recall watching it Saturday afternoons on "Superhost's Mad Theater" on Channel 43 in northeast Ohio when I was a kid. *The Blob* was shot in and around Phoenixville, Pennsylvania, a small town thirty miles northwest of Philadelphia. The climactic scene of the film is staged in downtown Phoenixville at the Colonial Theater, where hundreds of people run screaming from the movie theater as the Blob attacks inside.

Following its Hollywood moment, the Colonial Theater had several more years of success but changes in the movie theater industry made theaters like it—single screen, located downtown—into an endangered species. The theater changed hands numerous times over the years but was eventually purchased by the city in 1996 with the hopes of repurposing it as a community theater. The following year, local residents formed the Association for the Colonial Theater (ACT) to raise money to rehabilitate the theater. One of the association's most successful fundraisers was a special $100 per seat screening of *The Blob* in the original theater. People flocked to the event, and the association successfully re-opened the theater in 1999. The following year, they screened *The Blob* again, and again local viewers went crazy over the opportunity to see the movie inside the Colonial. In response, the group even worked with the audience to re-create the famous scene of fleeing the theatre from the Blob—and a new ritual and tradition was born.

Blobfest occurs every July and has grown bigger each year. The original film and the communal run out of the theatre are the centerpieces of a three-day festival that features classic horror films, pop culture, food and music. Attendance for the 2013 event topped 5,000 people, and Mary Foote, now executive director of The Colonial Theater, credits the theater and *The Blob* with the economic resurgence of downtown Phoenixville. She noted that the city has "grown organically like the Blob" over the past decade and that the Colonial was the cornerstone that started the process. The theater draws 500,000 people to downtown Phoenixville on an annual basis.

Many cities have their version of the Colonial theater, but few have been as successful as the Colonial in regaining a following. As silly as it sounds, the Colonial owes much of its success to the Blob. The classic B-movie connection gives the Colonial an "X-factor" that other theatres don't have. Apparently many folks share my love for *The Blob*, and for them the opportunity to visit the theater and, better yet, watch the film in the location of its most thrilling scene—talk about a meta moment!—has grown into a beloved city ritual and tradition. Every city has a strange factoid or pop culture connection that could become an element in shaping identity, if it is seen as a future building block and not just a historical footnote.

ANN W. RICHARDS CONGRESS AVENUE BRIDGE, AUSTIN, TEXAS

The Ann W. Richards Congress Avenue Bridge, also known as the South Congress Bridge, in Austin is home to North America's largest urban bat colony.[1] From March through October, the bridge shelters an estimated 1.5 million Mexican free-tailed bats, which migrate to Mexico for the winter. Each summer night, hundreds of people will gather on the bridge and on the shores of Lady Bird Lake to watch as the bats emerge at dusk. As soon as the sun sets, the bats stream out from under the bridge in search of food. An estimated 100,000 tourists come to see the bats each year, and a 1999 research study estimated that the bats had an annual impact of nearly $8 million on Austin's economy.[1]

In October 2013, I visited the bridge and was able to experience the bats first-hand. Even on a Thursday evening, hundreds of people gathered to see the spectacle, which did not disappoint. At first the bats start to trickle out, then quickly formed a veritable fire hose of creatures emerging from under the bridge. Clouds of them moved across the lake and become visible against the illuminated Austin skyline in a strangely beautiful display. This ritual and tradition illustrates an important concept—turning a negative into a positive.

Most people don't like bats. In fact, we typically refer to bats as rats with wings. When most people discover a bat colony, they call animal control. But bats get a bad rap. It turns out each one consumes thousands of insects a night, especially mosquitoes, and they are plant pollinators for the local environment. Despite popular myth, bats have yet to bite a human on the neck! So the fact that Austin has embraced the bats, making them an unofficial city mascot as well as a beloved tradition, reveals how we might rethink perceived negatives in our own places. With a little creative judo, we can turn those negatives into positives.

PUMPKIN ROLL, MONTAGUE, MICHIGAN

Montague, Michigan, is a small town (population 2,361) on the west coast of the state on the banks of Lake Michigan. My friend Janelle Mair grew up in Montague, and she related the following local ritual and tradition. Every October when she was growing up, local kids would go into the neighborhoods and steal pumpkins. They would load them into the backs of pickup trucks, take the pumpkins to the top of a small hill in downtown Montague and bowl them down the street into cars and storefronts below. This became known as "rolling." Mair laughed when she told me this, saying "Hey, we were young, and it was a small town." Obviously this was a negative behavior that the community wanted to discourage. After years of trying to fight it, the former chief of police decided to sanction the roll. Over fifteen years ago, the city created Pumpkinfest, which occurs in October before Halloween. For a dollar, you can buy a pumpkin and bowl it down the street, which is lined with hay bales. Today, the hill includes ramps and targets for even more interactivity. In October 2013, nearly one thousand people participated in the daylong Pumpkinfest celebration. Here is another great example of taking a negative behavior, getting creative and turning it into a positive.

INTO THE COMMUNITY LAB

As we experiment with our communities, rituals and traditions are excellent starting points to build from and around. As we consider new projects and efforts, here are some principals and guidelines that we would do well to consider. Again, these are not prescriptive but rather suggestive of some of the ways we might think about a given problem.

EMBRACE TEMPORARY

In our efforts to build better cities, we typically envision big, community-defining projects. We also envision these projects as being permanent, or at least long-term. That is all well and good, but big and long-term projects require lots of time and resources. Anything that is going to stand for decades is going to invite extensive community discussion and perhaps some hesitation about commitment. Every city has had the experience of trying to build consensus around a major project. Such projects are like committing to a long-term relationship; they are like getting married. At the other end of the spectrum are temporary projects, often small but not exclusively so, which are limited to a finite duration from the outset. These temporary projects allow for much more experimentation than permanent ones. People are far more likely to approve a new and experimental project or approach if they know they can undo it later. Temporary tattoos and Las Vegas exist for this very reason.

When mayor Michael Bloomberg and Department of Transportation Director Janette Sadik-Khan of New York City announced their intention to make Times Square into a pedestrian-only zone that would ease traffic and midtown congestion, they did so on a temporary basis.[xiv] In May 2009, Bloomberg noted, "We are going to closely monitor the results to determine if this pilot works and should be extended beyond its trial period."[xv] For many, including local businesses, the thought of closing the street to traffic was a horrible idea. People predicted massive traffic jams and loss of business, a reaction that Bloomberg had anticipated, which is why he eased into it as a temporary pilot program.

The first changes to the square were merely painted directional lines, orange cones and flower boxes to alter the traffic routes. The city then brought in inexpensive lawn chairs and spread them around the area. At first New Yorkers were amused, but they quickly realized how much better the experience of a pedestrian center in the heart of the city was for them. In July 2010, Mayor Bloomberg announced that the pilot program would become permanent. By that time, local merchants, who had initially opposed the change, were more than 70 percent in support of the project.[xvi] People needed to see it, to experience it before they could fully appreciate it, and by making it temporary, Bloomberg allayed their fears and allowed them to come to love it in their own time.

GRANARY ROW, SALT LAKE CITY, UTAH

Salt Lake City has wide streets. Really wide streets that harken back to when city founder Brigham Young declared that the streets needed to be wide enough "for a team of four oxen and a covered wagon to turn around."[xvii] Ox carts are not known for their nimble turning radius, and as a result Salt Lake City has some canyon-wide streets that cars love but which make for dangerous crossings for pedestrians and an overall dissipation of energy in the heart of the city's downtown. Redoing the streets would be a smart but excruciatingly inconvenient and expensive process, so in early 2013 Salt Lake City decided to turn this negative factor into a potential positive.

The Kentlands Initiative is a community led non-profit that has been operating in the community since 2009 and focuses on redeveloping the Granary District. During a public planning workshop in 2012, the idea for Granary Row was born. In the middle of the 700 South block in the Granary District, just on the outskirts of downtown, the group created a temporary performance, retail and gathering space called Granary Row. It debuted in June 2013 and remained in place through November. The city used recycled materials such as shipping containers to create its stage, retail kiosks and a beer garden. And Granary Row literally sits in the middle of a very wide street. As with Times Square, using some paint and minimal directional lines, Salt Lake City carved out a third space in the midst of traffic. It looked like a small version of Brooklyn's famous (now closed) Dekalb Market.

James Alfandre, executive director of the Kentlands Initiative, told me that placing Granary Row in the middle of a wide street demonstrated how the neighborhood's underutilized resources could be reclaimed for "human-centered growth and activity."[xviii]

"There's an untapped wealth of opportunity in the roadway," said Christian Harrison, also from the Kentlands Initiative. "Here we are developing the center of the road in a way that serves the community it's in and also for the future."[xix]

Photo courtesy of Kentland Initiative

Open every Thursday and Friday night and all day Saturday, Granary Row drew hundreds of people after work for music, beer and local retail. Designed to help revive the business and residential culture of the area, Granary Row also served as an experimental space where creative entrepreneurs and artists could showcase their talents economically. It was a successful experiment, and the Kentland Initiative plans to stage it again in 2014.

With the project, Salt Lake City did two important things. First, the city tried something new that could easily have failed. And so what if it did? There were relatively few costs involved in building Granary Row, and the community would have learned something in the process. Second, it succeeded in taking a negative (excessively wide streets) and turning the same factor into a positive, which is a lesson that cities everywhere should consider. If we are able to look at existing problems differently and try a creative, temporary solution, we might find many more opportunities in our community than are immediately apparent.

A BETTER BLOCK, DALLAS, TEXAS

Temporary is also a way to challenge long established rules and regulations without running headlong into reflexive opposition. If you ever looked at your city's rules and regulations around public usage, you would find a tangled web of overlapping, outdated and even conflicting regulations that are most likely contrary to the overall goal of a better city. But the city's administrative fiefdoms will vigorously defend those rules because it is what they have always done.

The Better Block Project (betterblock.org) was formed in Dallas, Texas, in April 2010 by Jason Roberts and Andrew Howard, who were inspired by the possibilities of temporary usage and breaking some rules. Roberts and Howard began working in their own neighborhood by taking an under-utilized block and transforming it over a weekend into a "better block" by installing seating, landscaping, pop-up restaurants and shops, performance spaces and even temporary bike lanes (unofficial, of course). Their goal was to engage the local community in building something together but also to demonstrate dramatically to official city makers what was possible. Roberts told me that they intentionally invited city officials and department leaders to the project and highlighted all the rules they broke in creating the better block. Their point was to urge the same officials to re-examine the city's rules and ask what needed to be changed and amended to allow the city to achieve better spaces. Their plan worked. Better Block was able to get the city code amended and made more flexible for 21st century uses such as pop-up retail, street performance and food trucks.

FILL THE GAPS

In my talks, I regularly challenge audiences to step up and fill in the gap "between the city we desire and the city we can afford." The idea being that instead of waiting for others to make the city better for us, we should engage and do something, even a small thing, that makes our places better. It's a simple premise but one that has been particularly timely over the past few years as cities have wrestled with budgetary challenges.

This kind of gap filling, or temporary thinking, has achieved new heights in Christchurch, New Zealand. Following the devastating earthquakes of 2010 and 2011, citizens there have responded with an amazing array of creative projects. One of the most famous is the Re:Start Mall in the Christchurch central business district. When the heart of the downtown retail district was destroyed in the earthquake, the city recognized that it could be years before the retail center could be rebuilt. The city's Property and Business Owners group came up with an idea to "restart" the heart of the city via its retail district. In October 2011, Re:Start Mall opened with twenty-seven shops and cafes, primarily housed in quickly assembled and designed shipping containers. The brightly colored containers offered a reason to come back downtown and shop as well as sense of hope and a return to normal. The city noted that the containers could be easily moved or transitioned into permanent structures in the future. Other pop-up cafes, retail and restaurants inspired by Re:Start's style and success have appeared all over the city.

The organization Gap Filler, also from Christchurch, has taken this premise and applied it to many vacant spaces in the city following the devastating earthquakes. Their approach is ingenious; they seek to activate empty spaces with temporary, creative interventions such as outdoor dance mats, bicycle-powered cinemas, murals and even an amazing performance space created entirely from wooden shipping palettes. Unlike the major undertaking of Re:Start Mall, the projects Gap Filler instigates are on a scale that engages everyday citizens in the process. Their notoriety has even inspired general use of the term "gap fillers" for this type of project, which has spread all over the region.

"We started Gap Filler after the earthquakes... to bring life, energy, positivity, creativity to vacant sites in Christchurch and to connect everyday people with their city here and now," said Coralie Winn, one of the co-founders of Gap Filler.[xx] Making everyday citizens part of the process has been key. Gap Filler provides the legal and insurance elements that can deter ordinary citizens from undertaking public projects, thus re-moving one of the main barriers to citizen action. Gap Filler notes, "there are wonderful ideas for the future city, but that's a long way off and many people need reasons to stay now. Gap Filler gives everyday people a way to contribute to the city's regeneration instead of passively waiting for the professionals to do the job."[xxi]

TARGET UNUSED SPACES

You don't need to suffer from a disaster to have empty lots and vacant storefronts in your city. Sometimes you just end up with an odd lot that defies development. In July 2012, I was in Pensacola, Florida, where I was shown an empty lot in the city's downtown at the corner of Palafox and Main Streets. The parcel was only about twenty-five feet wide but about one hun-dred and fifty feet deep; it would clearly take a uniquely shaped business to fill it. My guide related that the city had secured short-term rights to use the lot and was going to bring in four Airstream trailers to create a food truck food court. The city would install picnic-style seating and build restrooms, but that was the extent of their involvement. They wanted to put the land to some productive use and if they got a tenant interested in a long-term lease of the space, it would not be hard to move four trailers. The food court would be a temporary gap filler, but it could end up lasting for years. Called Al Fresco, the project opened in early 2013 and has become a major hotspot in downtown Pensacola.

Take an inventory of your community's empty and unused spaces, especially the odd or unique ones. They are all potential launching pads for something cool. We fixate on a particular way of seeing a space, often to the exclusion of other ideas that don't fit within our preconceived notions. By allowing creative people and entrepreneurs to experiment in these spaces, we may discover uses that we never believed possible. At the very least, we inject some life and energy into moribund places, knocking the dust off and reminding the community that a heart still beats there.

FIND YOUR SIGNATURE EVENT

Every city wants a signature event that is an economic force as well as a solidifier of community identity. Cities look enviously at South by Southwest (SXSW) in Austin, Mardi Gras in New Orleans, the Sundance Film Festival in Utah or even Comic-Con in San Diego. These are signature events that have become synonymous with their places. They also lure in bounties of tourists and money. Consequently I hear all the time about how places are trying to find a signature event. But too often I hear that they want to do their own version of SXSW. I think SXSW is amazing, and maybe the world does need another music-film-tech festival. But even if you can pull off a great SXSW-style event, you are at best producing a great copy that will inevitably be compared to the original event and the original place.

This is not to say that you cannot import an event and make it your own. In Miami Beach, the city was able to partner with the well-known and long established Art Basel art fair in Switzerland, and in 2002 Miami Beach debuted Art Basel Miami

Beach. The annual event has become a premier arts and cultural attraction for the city, furthering the growth of other cultural institutions including art museums and galleries. Hong Kong got on the bandwagon, and in 2013 that city debuted Art Basel Hong Kong. Importing an event is an option, and sometimes you can be the beneficiary of an event's expansion into your city.

Gen Con, the now world-famous gaming convention, had very humble beginnings in Lake Geneva, Wisconsin. In 1968, Gary Gygax, the co-creator of Dungeons & Dragons, started the first convention. Over the years the convention grew and moved all over Wisconsin but eventually settled on a permanent home in Milwaukee in the mid 1980s. Sadly for Milwaukee, the convention outgrew the city's convention center in the 21st century, and Gen Con moved to its current home of Indianapolis in 2002. Since coming to Indianapolis, the convention has more than doubled in size to nearly 56,000 attendees (including me) in 2014. Indianapolis has embraced the convention and made it a signature event. While perhaps not on a par with the Indy 500, Gen Con is the second largest convention hosted by the city each year.

In 2012, I visited San Diego and had an opportunity to speak with then-mayor Jerry Sanders (not the grabby one—the mayor prior to him). We were at San Diego's convention center, and I mentioned that I wanted to come back someday to attend Comic-Con, the world famous comic book and pop culture event held every August. As we stood amidst the huge convention center, Mayor Sanders told me that the city was committed to further expanding the facilities as Comic-Con continues to grow and demand ever more space. Rather than go the way of Milwaukee, Mayor Sanders recognized how important Comic-Con was to the community both in economic terms and in terms of identity. Comic-Con is a perfect example of a local, seemingly obscure event that grew into something amazing.

The San Diego Comic Book Convention, commonly known as Comic-Con, began in 1970 with 300 attendees. In 2013, it hosted over 130,000 attendees for a five-day event and generated an estimated $180 million in local economic impact.[xxii] While most events will never reach these heights, examples like Comic-Con provide us with an important lesson in value of seemingly niche, locally grown events. Instead of looking to emulate some other place, cities would do well to take a careful inventory of their own quirky events and perhaps try to support and expand them.

In the fall of 2013, I was in Huntsville, Alabama, and had a chance to discuss the idea of signature events with some of the community's leadership. While touring Lowe Mill, an old textile factory that has been converted to a massive arts and entertainment complex, we happened upon a shop that was selling custom made cigar box guitars. I had never seen these handcrafted instruments, but their history dates back to the 1840s, when people would make four-stringed guitars using the wooden cigar box as the resonating chamber of the instrument. I was amazed, and my hosts mentioned that Huntsville had been hosting an annual cigar box music festival for the past several years. Right there I stopped and said, "That is your signature event."

The Flying Monkey Arts Cigar Box Guitar Festival started in 2005 and has seen steady growth ever since then. The latest incarnation brought in hundreds of attendees from all over the U.S. and several other countries. Perhaps because the event seemed very niche market-oriented (but so are gaming and comic books) and its numbers were not as significant as the local CVB might like, the event had not received the consideration it should have.

Locals were, of course, happy to have the festival but did not necessarily see it as a true signature event for the city. But to my outsider eyes, the event fit wonderfully into Huntsville's maker culture. Known as Rocket City, Huntsville is home to a huge number of engineers, scientists and other makers of things. It would be an easy step to expand the cigar box festival to include more maker events and culture. Just as SXSW grew by adding complimentary elements—first film, then technology—to its original core, so too could the Cigar Box Guitar Festival grow into something nationally and even globally known for Huntsville.

TRY A LITTLE COLOR

Color theory invites consideration of the role that colors play in creating identity, mood and emotions. When we design our interior spaces, we are highly conscious of this process, trying to create just the right feelings in the places we inhabit the most. For some older cities, color schemes have developed over hundreds of years. Jodhpur, India, is known as the "Blue City" because of the brightly painted blue houses that surround the historic Mehrangarh Fort. Charles Landry observes in his book *The Sensory Landscape of Cities* that Marrakesh, Morocco, is pink, while Bologna, Italy, is dominated by burnt red rooftops and Izamal in the Yucatan Peninsula of Mexico is predominantly mustard yellow. These color schemes were set in motion hundreds of years ago and were sometimes due to available pigments as much as conscious choice. In other cases, certain colors were used for specific reasons. Blue for example, is a much more difficult color to produce and so was used by the ancient Egyptians to indicate divinity, while the Romans used it as a primarily decorative color.

For modern cities, color is generally an ad hoc process resulting in a kaleidoscope of shades that blend together in the best cases (in the worst, there's a jarring effect where colors collide). Some places are able to incorporate a color design element that becomes a unifying theme in the grand scheme of the city. Melbourne, Australia, made a concerted effort to use locally sourced bluestone for its sidewalks. Over the past two decades or more, the city has gradually increased the number of bluestone sidewalks to the point that they now cover almost the entire downtown core. Similarly, in Rio de Janeiro you know you are on the famed Copacabana Beach by the distinct black-and-white tiles that form the walkways. The residents of Juzcar, Spain, a very small village near Malaga, agreed to paint all their homes blue in 2011 to promote a Smurfs movie. Although Sony offered to repaint the town, the 220 residents voted to stay blue. Tourism to the town grew from a few hundred visitors the year before to over 80,000 in the year after going blue.[xxiii]

Color impacts our emotional states and offers a simple opportunity to improve community spirits. Charles Landry first shared with me this story about Tirana, Albania. In 2000, a left-wing painter named Edi Rama was elected mayor of Tirana, a city that was struggling to shrug off years of Iron Curtain planning and development. The city was very broke and very broken—running water was available only for a few hours each day. One of Rama's early efforts was to order three percent of the city's budget to be spent on brightly colored paint that was used to cover many of the dilapidated and depressing buildings with boldly hued designs. He could not afford to fix or even tear down these eyesores, but he made them remarkably colorful, artistic and even fun. The city's building façades became a modernist gallery and this launched a long, successful run for Rama who served as mayor until 2011. In 2013, he was elected Prime Minister of Albania. There is power in a coat of paint.

In my own travels, two extremes have come into view: Goleta, California, and Gulfport, Florida. Goleta is a city of 30,000 adjacent to Santa Barbara on the coast of California.

Their traditional downtown neighborhood, called Old Town, is located on Hollister Avenue. I heard from officials there about their need to revitalize this part of town. They wanted better retail and more restaurants to bring back this historic district. As I walked around the neighborhood, I was struck by the monochrome surfaces of the buildings. Nearly every building was painted a dark, bland brown. Even the local Wendy's, usually known for its bright red exterior, was painted the same brown. I asked the leadership whether this was intentional, but they said no; the neighborhood had unconsciously adopted the dull color scheme over time. I suggested that "Old Town Brown" needed to be replaced with some much more vibrant colors. An injection of color would be a cheap and easy way to signal that new energy was coming and to help kick-start the further redevelopment of the neighborhood.

Gulfport, Florida, is a small artistic community at the southern tip of Pinellas County. It is known for restaurants, boat docks and for its impressively colorful buildings. Gulfport is the opposite of Goleta. Over the years, some artistic people painted their houses and businesses with bold color combinations, which in turn challenged others to paint their buildings. Walking around Gulfport recently, I even saw some beautifully painted manhole covers. Gulfport residents have created a vibrant visual identity that you cannot ignore. I call it the most colorful city in Florida and certainly one of the most distinct. The wonderful colors create a mood and atmosphere that locals and tourists alike cannot help but be influenced by. Both of these examples occurred naturally over time, but I would challenge communities to consciously think about color and be intentional about its uses and potential.

A VIKING FUNERAL

In addition to serving as the state capital, Sacramento, California, is home to the National Basketball Association franchise the Kings. The team currently plays in an arena located a few miles outside of town. In 2013, the franchise was sold to a new ownership group that was committed to keeping the team in Sacramento. As part of the deal, a new arena was to be built, and the site selected was in downtown Sacramento between Old Sacramento and the capital area on a decaying urban mall called the Downtown Plaza. The mall closed in May 2014 and will be demolished by year's end.

When I spoke in Sacramento in early 2014, the city was both relieved that the team was staying and excited about the prospect of a new downtown arena. During my conversations there I raised the idea of doing something fun and memorable to send off the old Downtown Plaza. Whenever a building closes for the final time, there is always a short window of time before the wrecking ball or demolition teams arrive to make way for the next project. That time gap is interesting because you can pretty much do anything on the old site with no fear of ruining it. Want to have a giant paint ball fight? Stage a really loud concert?   Turn the space into a temporary skate park? All are viable ideas, since the building is coming down anyway. As we discussed the prospect, I talked about sending the Downtown Plaza out with bang, to which one of the leaders of the city's young professional organization said the occasion sounded like "a Viking funeral." To which I exclaimed, "Yes! Just like a Viking funeral!"

The next time a building is scheduled for demolition in your community, take advantage of the opportunity to use the space as a venue. The creative people in your community will be chomping at the bit to get in and do something wild and wonderful. When do they ever get a canvas so grand and so destructible? This not only sends the building off in style, it opens up the creative possibilities of the next space as well.

LOVE CAMPAIGNS

One of the most obvious and straightforward tactics that many cities have begun to use is their version of a "love campaign." This can be a simple as a Facebook page or a Twitter hashtag. Some love campaigns may have political or economic underpinnings, such as Love Lakeland (Florida), which was instigated by a local businessman and his wife as a component of his political campaign for mayor. They also owned a promotional products company and were able to produce and distribute a wide variety of items printed with the message "Love Lakeland." The campaign helped raise his visibility and, in late 2013, Howard Wiggs was elected mayor. In other cities, such as Muskegon, Michigan, such campaigns have self-organized and have impacted public policy and community branding (as we will see in Chapter 5). Of course, I think this is a great thing. Some may wonder if the proliferation of love campaigns everywhere will make the idea into a cliché. I hope not. Have we stopped writing love songs because thousands have come before? Does your partner ever get tired of hearing that you love him or her? Can you ever say "I love you" too much to those that matter most? I think not. Love campaigns will manifest in their own unique and local ways. They will ebb and flow and change over time, just like any relationship. They will always seem trite and clichéd to the cynical, and that is fine. Most of us want to live in a world where love matters and in a city that reflects that ideal back to us: A city that we can love and one that, in some strange, improbable way, loves us back.

Chapter Three
Love Hurts

Relationships take work, and the relationship that we have with our cities can be just as complex and demanding as the ones we have with friends and family. Emotions ebb and flow, and love doesn't always mean sunshine and roses. There are heartaches and setbacks along the way. This chapter looks at the hurts that come with loving a city—from the little things that irritate and annoy us to the big things that threaten to kill our love. When the stakes are high, feelings can be strong; as we try to build a better place, we can get battered and bloodied. These hurts leave scars that we forever carry forward, but they can also make us stronger and better caretakers of the places we love.

DAGGERS

The idea of the "love note," a small thing that has an out-sized impact on our emotional perception, has proven to have resonance with people all over the world. Once I explain the concept—no matter what city I'm in—people smile and immediately seem to grasp the idea with enthusiasm. Of course, they want in turn to share their community's love notes with me. But over the past few years, I also have heard over and over again about the small but painful and disheartening elements of city life. These "anti-love notes" have a correspondingly outsize impact on the way people feel about their places—in a negative sense. I call such occurrences "daggers" because they are the tiny, death-by-a-thousand-cuts annoyances that damage our relationships with our places. We don't realize how much damage these seemingly insignificant aggravations are doing to our relationship with our place, but over time they can accrue and fester into emotions that might trigger the demise of our civic relationship.

RED LIGHT CAMERAS

In 2011, my hometown of St. Petersburg, Florida, instigated a pilot program to install two dozen red light cameras around the city. The city government, like many others, had bought into the idea that the cameras, installed and maintained by a private company, would be a revenue source and increase safety by discouraging people from accelerating through yellow lights. In the first year of the program, St. Petersburg generated over $700,000 in revenue[xxiv] from citations at a rate of $158 per ticket. The State of Florida got its share, which amounted to over $1.8 million the first year, and the Arizona-based company that installs and maintains the systems for municipalities got its share as well. This revenue was lower than projected. Like other cash-strapped communities, St. Petersburg had to deal with not only with widespread public antipathy for the cameras but also the fallout from failed revenue projections. The cameras became a political issue in elections. Candidates were routinely asked where they stood on the issue of retaining the cameras, and in March of 2014 St. Petersburg's city council voted to remove the cameras by the end of the year[xxv].

Why is our knee jerk reaction to hate red light cameras when the vast majority of us are law-abiding citizens who are unlikely to get a ticket, especially when we understand that our cities are hard pressed for revenue? These programs offend us on two fundamental levels. First is the impersonal, "Big Brother" aspect of the camera that condemns us. Second is the disingenuous way such systems typically are sold to communities. Like a 21ˢᵗ century speed trap, they are a money grab for cities under the thin disguise of increased public safety, and citizens know it. In fact, evidence that the cameras increase safety is mixed, with some data even showing increased rear-end collisions as drivers brake suddenly at camera-monitored intersections out of fear of getting a ticket[xxvi]. When put to a public vote, no red light camera program has ever survived.[xxvii] I made the suggestion to former St. Petersburg Mayor Bill Foster that if he wanted to mitigate public antipathy for the cameras, the city could designate revenue from specific cameras for specific community services. For example, put charges originating from the red light at Fourth Street and 22nd Avenue into funding for the arts. Turn the Gandy Boulevard traffic light into funding for after-school programs. Then publicize how much money is channeled to those recipients by the cameras. By doing so, the city could at least connect the dagger of the red light camera to a recognized public good. People may never love the cameras, but acceptance for them might increase if citizens could see how revenue earned supports programs that they value.

BILLBOARDS & VISIBLE UTILITY LINES

Charles Landry, the author of *The Art of City Making*, calls billboards and visible utility lines "urban dandruff." They are ugly and annoying but not thought of as significant problems. But sometimes, more like a cancer cell than dandruff, one urban eyesore can metastasize into something that does threaten the entire city—because, like cancer, such things have a nasty habit of spreading. The first billboard that goes into an area makes it much easier and much more enticing for a second and third billboard. Then multiple billboards are competing for eyeballs, creating an arms race for attention that causes billboards to rapidly multiply. The same holds true with visible power lines. Once they are out in view, it is easy to justify hanging more of them until they loom over us like dour drapes. Cities are now trying to undo the decisions and public policy that allowed both eyesores to become so prevalent in our communities. Many cities are using the lure of new electronic billboards to remove older billboards that litter the landscape. In return for the ability to install one electronic billboard in an advantageous spot, the billboard company has to remove many older ones throughout the city. So, too, it goes with the painfully slow process of burying utility lines. Block by block, as updating existing cable and fiber optic lines become necessary, cities are using the work as an opportunity to clear older utility lines.

Though we become accustomed to pervasive ugliness in our communities, there is still a psychic and emotional cost to this negativity. We don't realize it, but such visual cues impact our actions, our attitudes towards each other and our work, and our overall feelings about ourselves. Like the "broken window theory" that applies to small, anti-social or criminal behaviors, these small psychic cuts, the daggers, accumulate over time and can bring people and their cities down. Each negative act makes the next easier, and this negative accounting can grow rapidly once it reaches a tipping point. We can repair our communities one act at a time by removing a billboard, hiding some power lines, cleaning up an empty lot, painting a mural over a graffiti-tagged wall or fixing a broken window.

HOLES IN THE FABRIC OF YOUR COMMUNITY

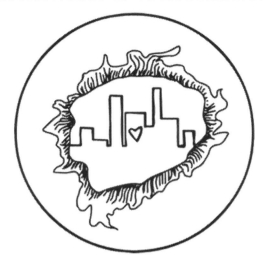

Every community has empty, vacant, under-utilized and generally unloved spaces. When those spaces occur in highly visible places, they become a hole in the fabric of the city. Holes become daggers because they are noticeable and persistent reminders of failures—a failure of the market, a failure of planning, a failure of leadership. And they can often linger for years.

In 1997, a real estate developer in Boise, Idaho, announced plans for the Boise Tower, a 22-story condo project in the heart of downtown. The project began well, but the developer quickly ran out of money. For the next 14 years, a literal giant hole in the ground, surrounded by chain link fence, marred the downtown Boise landscape. Fittingly, it became known as "The Hole," while the community struggled with what to do about the eyesore. I spoke with Boise Mayor David Beiter, and he told me that at every public event where he spoke during the first eight years of his time in office he would get questions about what to do about The Hole. That dagger became something more than a failed real estate project. The highly visible location and extreme duration of "The Hole" combined to impair progress all over downtown Boise. Noted Ken Gardner, chairman of the Utah-based Gardner Company, a real estate developer not associated with the original project: "There will never be confidence in downtown Boise as long as that hole exists."[xxviii]

The property changed hands numerous times until finally, in September 2011, Gardner's company purchased it and announced plans to build a 15-story office tower on the site, anchored by the company's Boise office as well as Salt Lake City-based Zions Bank. Ground broke on the project shortly afterward. When I visited Boise in early 2013, the building was nearly complete and preparing for a grand opening in the fall, to the delight of many city residents.

In Petoskey, Michigan, another failed hotel and condo development, "Petoskey Pointe," resulted in a similar giant hole in the heart of their urban core. It lasted for more than six years. Known by numerous appellations including "the Petoskey Pit," "the Hole" or simply "the Pit," this dagger ended up becoming the property of Northwest Michigan Bank via foreclosure. And therein lay the problem. The bank did not want to invest in maintaining the property as it sought a buyer for the land. As a result, the fences and walls around the Petoskey Pit became dilapidated—a worse eyesore even than they had been initially. Pressure from the city met with resistance from the bank, and it was not until the city decided to use safety regulations to compel the owners to mitigate the appearance of the hole that anything was done about the problem.[xxix] In May 2013, Northwest Michigan Bank announced plans to fix the fencing and partially fill the hole with sand. [xxx] Technically, the change was a victory for the city—but until something more substantive is done about the Pit, it will remain a dagger for Petoskey.

Petoskey and other cities that have their own versions of the Hole could take some inspiration from Lexington, Kentucky, and how that city dealt with a similar situation. CentrePointe was and remains a one square block development in the heart of downtown Lexington. The initial plan for its construction in 2008 called for a 35-story high rise with surrounding retail. The project was scheduled to be completed in mid-2010 as a centerpiece for the city, which was hosting the 2010 FEI World Equestrian Games. The World Equestrian Games is the Olympics of the equestrian world—and in Lexington, one of the global centers of the horse industry, its pending arrival was a huge deal. Thousands of well-to-do visitors were expected from all over the world, and the city was in the midst of massive preparations to shine.

The financial collapse of 2008 left many American development projects dead-in-the-water, and CentrePointe was one of them. The sting of the failure was exacerbated by the tie-in with the FEI Games and the fact that the developers of CentrePointe had razed a beloved entertainment block to make room for the fenced-in construction site that was becoming an embarrassment to the city. However, this time the developer, Dudley Webb, stepped up and got creative. In October 2009, Webb had turf and a traditional four-post horse fence installed all around the block.[xxxi] Thus the developer quickly and inexpensively turned the failed construction site into what appeared to be a downtown horse park. My friends in Lexington recounted how visitors during the games remarked how lovely it was that the city had a downtown horse park. As of early 2014, CentrePointe remains unconstructed but the grass and fencing remain, covering up and mitigating what could have been a significant hole in the fabric of downtown Lexington. A patch does not truly fix the hole, but sometimes an inexpensive patch can have a huge impact on the way the hole is perceived.

Lake Eola Park is the Central Park of Orlando, Florida. It is a beautiful green space with a round lake in the heart of downtown that often surprises visitors who think of Orlando as all theme parks and outlet malls. The fountain at the center of the lake was first installed in 1912, and then updated in 1957. By 2009, the fountain was by all accounts "showing its age."[xxxii] Limited functionality and rising maintenance costs (in excess of $50,000 per year) had many wondering about the future of the iconic structure. Then in August 2009, the fountain was struck by lightning, destroying the main pump and electrical controls. Worse yet, Orlando, like every other US city, was in the midst of the financial crisis that severely limited spending. The city would be hard-pressed to fund the repairs. Nonetheless, Orlando Mayor Buddy Dyer committed to not only fixing the fountain, but to updating it and making it even better than before.

"The Lake Eola fountain is much more than just a fountain. It's a symbol of our community and a source of pride for our residents," Dyer said. "So we are going to rebuild the Lake Eola fountain better than before."[xxxiii]" This was a bold move on the mayor's part because just a month prior to this decision the mayor and city council voted to reduce spending by $62 million and cut over 200 positions from the city, including 19 layoffs.

After a $2.3 million renovation, the fountain was rechristened on July 4, 2011, to much fanfare and celebration. Residents of Orlando told me that it was like turning a light back on inside their city. When the fountain was dark, something was missing—but when the fountain came back, bigger and better than ever, it was like the heart of the city was beating once again. The city's overall annual budget for public works is around $19 million. So depending on your point of view, $2.3 million is either a lot of money that could have been spent fixing potholes or a small price to pay for people to feel whole and positive about their city. One need only go to Lake Eola on a warm evening to see hundreds of people walking, biking, running or just sitting around the lake to see how valuable that beating heart is to the city.

Recall Gonzales, California, in Monterey County from chapter one. It is a small agricultural town (population 8,127) in what Californians call "the Salad Bowl" because so much of the nation's lettuce is grown in the area. The city's most notable feature is a green and white, golf ball-shaped water tower that sits at the heart of the city. At 125-feet tall, it is the tallest structure in town and bears the city name emblazoned across it. Because it is so visible from Highway 101, many people who have never been to the city know Gonzales because of the water tower.

In the past ten years or so, the paint on the water tower has faded badly, and the white "golf ball" looks as though it has been the victim of some very large birds. The tower needs some TLC, and its dilapidated condition has become a hole in the fabric of the community. To complicate matters, the older paint on the tower contained lead, so no simple paint job can be done. In fact, cleaning and repainting the tower necessitates that the entire structure be tented to prevent lead particles from escaping into the environment. The cost of such a project would be in excess of $400,000. While the city was seeking cost estimates on the cleaning project in 2013, one suggestion that arose was for the city simply to tear down the structure (a cheaper option than fixing it). The citizens of Gonzales spoke out and said that they wanted the tower restored, not removed, because it was a long-standing symbol of the community. The city confirmed that it would restore the tower, and it is slated for renovation in the spring of 2014.

While offering a series of talks and workshops in the region, I commented to Mayor Maria Orozco that when the tower is unveiled with its new paint job and pristine look, it would be a fantastic time for the city as a whole to sponsor a civic "spring cleaning." Using the attention that the tower is likely to receive, Gonzales could challenge itself to put on a new coat of paint everywhere and clean up the city, engaging citizens to add value to the project by improving their own private property. These types of galvanizing city moments don't happen every day, and I hope that Gonzales takes advantage of the opportunity and makes a significant event even more special by leveraging the positivity it will engender into something far bigger.

A final note about holes that hits close to home for me. In the fall of 2013, St. Petersburg, Florida voted to undo a massive public works project that would have removed an old, decaying municipal pier and erected in its place a new and elegant, albeit somewhat unusual, helix-shaped pier called "The Lens." The city had spent three years gathering public input, after which an international design competition led to a selection committee to choose a design for the new pier by Michael Maltzan Architects. But then some local residents decided that they did not like the unusual design, and they succeeded in initiating a referendum on whether to build the new design in August 2013. Though the city process of Maltzan's selection had been open and straightforward along the way, the citizen group decided to create a situation where the general public was essentially voting on whether it liked the design. On the day of the referendum, voters rejected the progressive design and its perceived expense. Their vote left a hole in the city fabric, because the existing pier had already been closed due to structural safety issues.

St. Petersburg now faces what Boise, Petoskey and others have faced. But what makes this situation so frustrating is that it was a self-inflicted wound. I personally liked The Lens design, but regardless of that I liked that the city was moving forward toward creating a new and iconic pier for all to enjoy. Recall that the citizens of Paris hated the idea of the Eiffel Tower when it was proposed. If they could have voted on it, the now famous monument perhaps would never have been built.

There will never be consensus on aesthetic issues. At best, design by committee usually results in something nobody hates. This fact was highlighted by renowned street artist Banksy, who wrote a scathing op-ed piece (that the New York Times rejected but became well known by circulating on-line) about the new One World Trade Center building. He called the building "104 floors of compromise," "the biggest eyesore in New York City" and "something they would build in Canada"[xxxiv] (Sorry, Canada—Banksy's words, not mine!) He summed up his disappointment by declaring the building was a giant sign saying, "New York – We lost our nerve." Ouch.

I suppose that sentiment is what I felt about the situation in St. Petersburg. We lost our nerve to move forward. The Pier became a referendum on the old versus the new, progress versus tradition—and progress lost. One local commentator has called the Pier a "ruin-in-waiting."[xxxv] As of this writing, the city is sorting out next steps, and all involved are promising to move forward with a new process hoped to lead quickly to new construction. I hope that happens, but I am sure the leadership in Boise said the same thing all those years ago.

HEARTBREAKERS

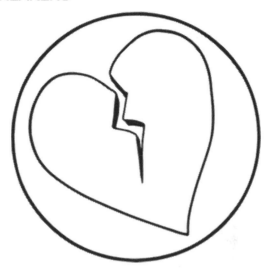

Some hurts go far beyond the painful daggers above. Some are truly injurious to people and their places and can take years to overcome, and even then are never forgotten. They can generate the massive wound that ends a place, or they can spur the unexpected rebirth that transcends prior history and puts the city on a new, albeit painful path.

JOPLIN, MISSOURI

On May 22, 2011, an enormous tornado, rated an EF5 (the most powerful and destructive type on the Enhanced Fujita Scale) ripped through Joplin, Missouri, resulting in the destruction of over 8,000 homes, hundreds of millions of dollars in damage, more than 900 injuries and 161 deaths. As in New Orleans in the aftermath of Hurricane Katrina, the Joplin community rallied and came together with a previously unknown sense of commitment and unity. "Restore Joplin" became a rallying cry and a promise to not give up on the city.

I visited Joplin almost two years to the day after the tornado. Jane Cage, a local entrepreneur turned city rebuilder, gave me a tour of the city. I saw many still-empty lots and a barren landscape with no trees. But I also saw lots of construction and a calming normalcy (in relative terms) in much of the city. I heard again and again from residents a prediction that the tornado would prove to be the most important incident in Joplin's history. Cage, a true Joplin co-creator and champion, summed the situation up beautifully when she noted that the tornado put Joplin on a new trajectory; instead of merely trying to maintain and hold steady, Joplin is on the rise and brimming with a confidence that the city did not have before. "The tornado was an opportunity we never asked for but can't afford to waste," she said to me as we passed through the treeless landscape.

Cage shared her sense, two years after the tornado, that the city's post-tragedy adrenaline was wearing off and that a resulting expiration of community spirit presented challenges for the city. She hoped that the cooperative sentiment engendered by the tornado would last, but as the city returned to its new normal, self-interest was beginning to reappear. I believe that the return of ordinary problems is a strange harbinger that things are working. As we drove around, Cage spoke about a traffic light being in full operation where it had been a blinking red and yellow for months. That's progress. Turns out that a key component of getting over the heartbreak of disaster is to get back towards a semblance of normal. As much as I joke about fixing potholes as a bare minimum standard for city building, there is comfort and success in the ordinary workings of our places.

THE FACTORY TOWN

Moraine, Ohio, is a small town (population 6,307) near Dayton in western Ohio. It has a long and prosperous manufacturing history that includes a nearly century long association with General

Motors. The first GM plant opened in Moraine in 1919 when GM produced airplanes. The plant became Frigidaire, a GM subsidiary, until 1979 when it reorganized as a truck plant. GM's operation in Moraine dominated the city's economy and identity. "It was always there, and it was always GM," said Moraine native and current city manager David Hicks. The relationship was a good one. Generations of workers and their families were tied to the plant, and many referred to the company as "Generous Motors" because of the high quality jobs and benefits it provided. But by the early 2000s, the American auto industry was in trouble, especially the makers of big SUVs and trucks. In early 2008, GM announced that it would be closing the plant permanently in December. On December 23rd, 2008, Moraine workers, their families and the community got a terrible Christmas present.

The official number of workers who lost their jobs in December 2008 is 2,170, but the cascade effect of the plant closing resulted in over 27,000 jobs lost across the region according to research conducted by the Institute for Research on Labor, Employment and the Economy (IRLEE) at the University of Michigan.[xxxvi] The closing of the plant was a potential death-blow for the city and much of the region. But Moraine did not die. Though the city did shed about 9% of its pre-plant closing population, shrinking to 6,316 residents, it has taken some important steps towards healing and moving forward.

I asked city manager David Hicks about the city's progress following the plant closure. He explained that at first the biggest hurdle was overcoming the mindset of denial adopted by many residents, who were convinced that GM was going to come back and that the closure was a ploy engineered by GM to break the unions. Getting the people of Moraine beyond that mindset required a huge amount of transparency on the city's part. People had to see the reality of the situation. So the city was open about budgeting issues, even forming a citizens budgetary advisory committee to solicit public input on the hard decisions that had to be made. All city employees agreed to a 10% pay cut, with the result that nearly every city job was spared, though Hicks did say that some positions were phased out or left unfilled when they became open. Hicks and the city became proactive about forming public-private partnerships in particular to support programs such as the city's Fourth of July celebration, which is now sponsored by a local business.

The city also had to decide what to do with the Pentagon-sized plant after GM left. (That's a big hole in the community fabric!) Most of the "developers" who expressed interest in the plant were actually scrappers, who wanted to raze the site for its materials and leave behind a barren, brown field with decades of chemical contaminants in it. Hicks and Moraine realized that trying to sell such an empty, depleted site would be nearly impossible in the future. Instead they fought to find a true redevelopment partner who would keep the facility and find uses for it.

The city of Moraine is now working with Industry Realty Group, a firm that specializes in industrial redevelopment, which has promised to find tenants and new uses for the mammoth facility. The former plant has been leased to five new companies that occupy over 10% of its vast space.[xxxvii] As of late 2013, nearly 200 jobs had returned to Moraine as a result of those companies. Though a fraction of its former glory, the importance of keeping the facility and finding new uses for it should not be underestimated. The plant "that was always there" will continue to be there for Moraine, as a link to its past and a possible bridge to the future.

CLEVELAND BROWNS

Compared to the loss of life and livelihood in Joplin and Moraine, the 1995 departure of the Cleveland Browns for Baltimore, Maryland, sounds insignificant. And by such a comparison, the loss of a sports team is insignificant. But in terms of damage to a population's sense of place and identity, "the Move," as Ohioans have come to know it, was one of the most tumultuous events in Cleveland's modern history.

The Cleveland Browns are one of the NFL's storied franchises, with historic roots that extend back to 1944. The team is best known for its first coach, Paul Brown, and its great Hall of Fame running back Jim Brown. Both just happen to share their last name with the team. For those of us who grew up in Northeast Ohio, the Browns are also known for heartbreaking disappointments on the field. ("The Drive and "The Fumble," both infamous last second losses against John Elway's Denver Broncos, come to mind.) But in 1995 the heartbreak was different because there was no consolation of saying, "We'll get 'em next year."

Browns owner Art Modell wanted a new stadium to replace the aging Cleveland Municipal Stadium, and he wanted the community to pay for it. Like so many other professional sports franchises before and since, he held the city hostage with the threat of moving the team. Modell successfully introduced the issue of a tax increase onto the November 1995 ballot, but then, true to the bitter irony that marks Cleveland sports, Modell preempted the vote by negotiating with the city of Baltimore. On November 6th, 1995, one day before the citizens of Cleveland would vote and pass by a sizable margin the public referendum to finance the new stadium, Modell announced that the team would move to Baltimore for the 1996 season.

Citizens were outraged and saddened. They truly felt betrayed by Modell. Steve Rushin, writing for *Sports Illustrated*, likened

Cleveland residents' collective reaction to the Browns' departure to the death of a family member.[xxxviii] People took the move personally to an incredible degree. The city, under the leadership of then-mayor Michael White, tried various ways to keep the team in Cleveland, including lawsuits and negotiations, but to no avail. Wisely, Mayor White did negotiate with the NFL to retain the team name, colors and history for a promised future expansion team. Three years of no football in Cleveland ended when the newly reconstituted Browns took the field on September 12, 1999. Even though the Pittsburgh Steelers immediately trounced the new team, it was a glorious day in Cleveland.

Cities everywhere in the U.S. felt the effect of the Browns leaving Cleveland. If Cleveland could lose the Browns, every city was in potential danger of watching their beloved team head for greener pastures. The city took a body blow to its collective psyche. Citizens felt it, and no doubt business and tourism felt it as well. The effect remains today as teams use the threat of moving to secure public funding for ever more elaborate facilities.

Seeking a positive side, I asked Ken Silliman, chief of staff to current Cleveland Mayor Frank Jackson, what was learned from the experience. Silliman was Development Chief for Mayor White at the time the Browns left. His reply was that Cleveland learned how to fight. Like many Midwestern cities, Cleveland had been on the losing side of economic and demographic shifts for a generation. In Midwestern fashion, the city had toughed it out. But the Browns showed that the city would fight for the things it believed in, especially if it felt wronged. Cleveland fought the move, and even though Modell successfully moved his team in the end, the city won unprecedented concessions from Modell and the NFL, which put a team back in place just three years later with its name, colors and history intact—a practice that has since become standard operating procedure for cities that lose their professional teams. Compare that achievement to the decades-long absence of professional football in Los Angeles, and you can see that while Cleveland lost the battle they won the war.

There has also been a lasting impact on the psyche of folks in Cleveland. My friends there relate a sense of gratitude and appreciation for not only the Browns but for many other aspects of their city. They lost something, and that hurt them. It made them angry, but then it made them love what they had even more. It takes a loss to make us fully appreciate what we have. Cleveland's 21st century resurgence, particularly in its downtown and University Circle, has origins in the lessons learned from the Browns departure and eventual return.

City building heartbreakers are complicated phenomena because they leave communities both stronger and weaker. Stronger because such occasions force us to change and adapt, stretch ourselves and prove we are more resilient than we believed. Heartbreakers remind us of what we value in our communities and to cherish what we have because it could go away. Weaker because, as tough and strong as we may become from the experience, we retain the scar that even years later may make us flinch when a similar circumstance arises. No one who experienced the Joplin tornado will ever not feel an extra twist in their stomach when a tornado siren goes off. When LeBron James left Cleveland for Miami in 2010, it reminded many of the loss they had experienced 15 years before. (See the postscript for update on LeBron and Cleveland.) This permanent scar can serve as a cautionary tale not to go down the road that led to the heartbreak, to do all we can to prevent the next one from happening and, most importantly, not to take for granted what we have in our community.

A SPECIAL NOTE ABOUT HEARTBREAK IN DETROIT

In July 2013, the city of Detroit filed for bankruptcy, trapped under the weight of $18 billion of debt with limited options. Many residents as well as outsiders had expected, and many more had dreaded, this turn of events. To some it was just another punch line in a long series of jokes at Detroit's expense. To others, it was a cautionary but seemingly inevitable tale relevant to the future of many cities. Outsiders took it as a death knell for the once-great city. But for the Detroit diehards who passionately love their decaying mess of a city, it was just another day in the D.

Detroit has its haters, and it certainly is a mess that could take years, perhaps even decades, to right. But so long as the city has people who still love it and believe in it, Detroit will never fail. That is the nature of love—it defies reason. But it absolutely matters. If the lovers of Detroit lost faith and hope in their city, then Detroit truly would be as screwed as many outsiders believe it to be. Sometimes passion, loyalty and evidence-defying faith in something are all that carry you forward. Detroit still has many amazing assets, including the revitalized auto industry and a toughness that comes from facing years of challenges. But one of the most important assets for that particular city—and for your city—is the love and devotion that its citizens have for it.

Few cities have been challenged in the way Detroit has, and its bankruptcy seems to be just another blow that its tough, passionate and prideful people will shrug off. The week after the bankruptcy announcement, Pure Detroit, one of the local pride t-shirt companies I wrote about in *For the Love of Cities*, sent an open letter to the city.

"For 15 years, we've had a savage love affair with this city. We've played matchmaker for many others along the way. And, like any

long-term relationship you give your whole heart to, there have been plenty of ups and downs...

But a love this strong isn't something you just give up on. We know a lot of our small business comrades, neighbors, friends and family in Detroit feel the same way. The news this week of bankruptcy doesn't make us forget the first time we fell in love with Detroit, serving hot chocolate outside of the David Whitney Building on Thanksgiving Day to parade patrons back in 1998. In fact, it only makes it stronger.

And because we know how self-conscious you can be sometimes, Detroit—you're still just as handsome as the first day we met you."[xxxix]

Mitch Albom, the award-winning journalist from Detroit, wrote: "Things may have collapsed under the weight of decades here, but we, the citizens of Detroit, have not. We still get up, go to work, kiss the kids, believe tomorrow could be better. We still call this place home. Proudly. Yeah, we're broke. But we're not broken. And if you know anything about us, you know this: We're not going anywhere."[xl]

Long live Detroit.

Chapter Four
Love Lessons

Somewhere between the grievous wounds and the highest of highs, we can learn a lot from loving our cities. Just as people have shared their love notes with me over the past few years, they have also talked about the hard lessons learned from their relationships with their places.

EXPECT A BACKLASH AGAINST BIKES

In *For the Love of Cities*, I made the case that a bicycle-friendly city is a lovable city. A bike-friendly city is healthier and more environmentally conscious—and most importantly, it sends a message to citizens that the city is not just about cars. In recent years, bike infrastructure, bike share programs and businesses and other bike-related projects have escalated dramatically as urban dwellers (especially younger ones) have begun looking for ways to ditch their cars. Major bike share projects in New York City and Chicago rolled out in late 2013. Bicycle commuting is on the rise by over 60% since 2000 and over 10% just between 2011 and 2012.[xli] All of this is great news. But I have heard from people all over the country about a corresponding backlash—or "bikelash" as the League of American Bicyclists calls it[xlii]—against bikes and cyclists as they become more prevalent. Angry motorists complain about cyclists ignoring traffic laws (which they often do), the CAVE people (Citizens Against Virtually Everything) complain about losing a couple of parking spaces, and the conspiracy theorists proclaim that cycling is the cover for a UN plot to take away your car. I thought the last idea was a joke until I ran into a few of its proponents in Arlington, Texas. Leaders in that city lamented the sad state of local politics, which had been hijacked by "Agenda 21" believers who equated any environmental or public transportation initiative with a sinister plan by the UN to take away their cars and guns and force them to live in Soviet-style block housing. When a plan for bike lanes was introduced in Arlington, opposition called the bike lanes everything from a socialist agenda to an evil plot against God-fearing automobile owners. Some argued that since cyclists did not pay gasoline taxes, they had no right to use the roads. In 2011, Arlington's city council narrowly voted to accept a bicycle master plan and, in late 2013, began the process of adding 4.4 miles of bike lanes to the city.[xliii]

Not all of the backlash against bikes is as absurd as what played out in Arlington. In 2011, I heard former Washington, D.C., mayor Adrian Fenty speak about his single term in office (2007-2010). When asked what lessons he had learned, of course he referenced the controversial policies on education that put him at odds with D.C. teachers and their union—it was the high profile issue that distinguished his administration. But he also referenced the significant backlash caused by the bicycle infrastructure that the city put in place during his administration.

To most people, a bike lane is seen as a sign of progress. But Fenty noted that to many longtime District residents, particularly the African-American community, bike lanes signaled gentrification. Such residents did not perceive the bike lanes as intended for their use and saw the hipsters on bikes in the lanes as a sign that the District was changing. The District, they feared, was becoming less of a place for them and more a place for new, privileged urban dwellers who have the luxury of choosing to ride their bikes to work. Whether this characterization was fair, the feeling was out there, and Fenty said it contributed to his loss of the African-American vote in his re-election bid. He noted that he should have made a better case from the beginning as to why the bike lanes were good for longtime residents of the District and not just the gentrifying newcomers.

Fenty's lesson is one that all of our cities would do well to remember. Basic progress and seemingly positive changes are not universally viewed as good things. In fact, such changes can be frightening to many, and we need to be patient with those who are afraid and help them see how change can and will benefit them. Our less enthusiastic neighbors might not be buckling on a helmet or putting on spandex to ride, but they can be more tolerant and accepting as they share the roads with their fellow citizens.

Confession: I used to ride bikes as a triathlete and a road racer. I took part in those annoying groups of riders who take up road lanes and all too often disregard road rules. I understand that cyclists piss off drivers. I get annoyed with them, too. But I think the overall backlash is due to the increased numbers of bikes and their visibility in our cities. Suddenly there are more cyclists on the road than we are used to seeing. And like selfish children, we are not used to sharing the road with anything other than other cars. We must learn new behaviors. Having to change creates resentments. This backlash is part of the natural process of finding a new equilibrium in our shared space. I suspect that early car owners met with similar antipathy from horse carriage drivers. More cyclists are coming—it's as inevitable as a $5 gallon of gas. Once drivers see more of them and get used to their sometimes maddening ways, they will accept that cyclists are part of the new normal of the roadways.

WHAT DO YOU MEAN "COMMUNITY ENGAGEMENT?"

I was recently on a conference call with clients in preparation for a visit to their community. They told me that their city manager had declared 2014 the year of "community engagement." The city had themed previous years in order to give some focus to their work; prior years had emphasized public safety and parks and recreation. What struck me was that I had been in contact with local activists in the city and was aware of some of the wants and needs that the activists had articulated, which were different from the city's desires and expectations in some cases. Both sides were talking about community engagement, and both sides were clearly passionate about the subject. What struck me, though, was the actual gulf that exists between what each of these points-of-view—city and citizen—understands by the term "community engagement."

Every city will acknowledge its desire to increase and improve community engagement. To a city, this typically means more input during sanctioned public forums. It means more volunteers for the street cleanup. It means more active neighborhood associations. All of these elements are great—safe, tidy and largely undisruptive to the city's plans. This type of engagement allows the city to move along as it had already planned, without any of the spontaneous messiness that can potentially accompany deeper, citizen-led community engagement. Those city activists, many of whom are co-creators in their community, are not content with the sanctioned manifestations of engagement. They have their own ideas about what they want to do. Often these ideas are at odds with the rules and regulations of the city and sometimes even go against the explicit plans and desires of the city. These highly engaged citizens will show up with their own ideas and an ability to make something happen, leaving many city managers to say "Hold on, we did not mean *that* kind of community engagement!"

This is the gap that exists between city and citizen in community engagement. Many citizens are content to channel their civic pride into traditional, sanctioned channels. Their efforts should be applauded. But a growing cadre of independent minded citizens is answering the call of engagement in different ways, powered by tools and technology as never before. They are, depending on your point of view, either the fly in the ointment or the missing X-factor for community success. I think they can be both.

For cities in dire need of resources and help, these citizens are a potential boon. Be it gap-filling projects or simple love notes, their contributions are the unplanned variable that could have remarkable impacts when properly activated (more on this later). Citizen activists can be a visible reminder to the broader community that creative, innovative people still care about the city. On the other hand, they can also be the unplanned variable that messes up long-established plans and efforts by the city—perhaps not intentionally, but well-meaning citizens don't always have all of the information that the city possesses, and they may inadvertently move against city efforts with their work. Cities need to do a balancing act; they need to ask themselves about the benefits and upside of this type of community engagement versus the potential pitfalls. I believe that it is not a hard calculus. True community engagement brings into play a whole other dimension of creativity, innovation and potential resources for the city. Such ideas and resources probably would not have entered into the mix had the city been more authoritarian in its approach to community. Co-creators think up ideas that the establishment might never consider. Rogue activists can create diversity of thought and action that is absolutely necessary for a community to remain creatively vital and innovative.

To close this gap of perception on the issue of community engagement we need to first admit that it exists. Such self-reflection can be difficult. Vince Long is the county administrator for Leon County, Florida, where the state capital city of Tallahassee is located. In the midst of the economic recession of 2012, Long and his staff administered what seemed to be a productive series of citizen engagement projects. The projects included bi-monthly educational events such as an interactive board game to illustrate the budgeting process to citizens, as well as a Lego-based session to simulate decision-making around the planning approval process. The series received national acclaim, yet Long felt the events still were not reaching deep enough into the community's heart and soul. "Many people participated and seemed to genuinely enjoy and learn a lot from the sessions. The national attention was great, but what we learned was that we were really just scratching surface of tapping into the talent, ideas, and resources that our citizens had to give. We were not content with checking a box for citizen engagement, so we had to ask ourselves—where do we go next?" Long said.

Long partnered with Village Square, a Tallahassee-based non-profit known for its own innovative approaches to civic engagement, including the event "Speed Date Your Local Officials." Long and Village Square executive director Liz Joyner did not want more of what they called "eat-your-broccoli" style community engagement. They took their inspiration from Benjamin Franklin's Club of Honest Whigs – an 18th century group that encouraged honest discussions among neighbors. The Club of Honest Whigs is credited with ideas such as volunteer firefighters and public libraries. What also is interesting about the Club of Honest Whigs is that their meeting place in London was St. Paul's Coffeehouse. (Co-creators were meeting up in coffee shops long before Starbucks existed!)

Tallahassee's city-supported Club of Honest Citizens debuted in the spring of 2014. The group held three events, all built around provocative questions such as "Is the public library dead?" or "Should government pay to bring business to town?" The city did not host these events in council chambers or typical meeting facilities. It staged them in a local bar over drinks and appetizers, at a pot-luck dinner hosted by a church and, in homage to Franklin, at a local coffee shop. Long said he realized that the resulting discussions might challenge some of his office's established plans and priorities, but the social interaction and exchange of new ideas was more important to him than maintaining the status quo.

Each event attracted over 40 people. Long indicated that the discussion was unusually candid and productive, and that new faces showed up to the meetings. The social settings seemed to have the desired effect. The group voted to start a $500 micro grant program ($500 is a magic number!), and their first project was to fund a special community dinner under a canopy-covered road. Long and Joyner hope to continue the process and engage more honest citizens in the discussions.

We all have the best intentions for our places and believe that more community engagement will be a benefit. From there we need to accept that engagement may take unexpected forms. We as citizens should consider that we may not have the full picture, and that our leadership may have good and sound reasons for taking the approaches they take. What is required is a bit of trust on both sides. Trust can be hard won, and trust can be quickly lost. Let's recognize the mutual benefits of trust and applying multiple visions of community engagement in our places. What will also be required is a bit of forgiveness from the city. It is inevitable that an engaged citizen will step beyond the lines, break some rules and cause a stir. The city needs to be reasonably forgiving, especially if the intent was good and the effort just. We don't want to squelch enthusiasm for the future of our cities, but we need to instill in residents a sense of boundaries and, dare I say it, rules. A deft touch and a willingness to experiment, such as Leon County demonstrated, is needed.

STOP CHASING COOL – "BECAUSE IT'S DENVER, MAN!"

I have heard many times in recent years that cities are trying to become "cool" in order to attract young talent. While I applaud the notion, I have to say that most efforts of this type have been off-target. From the regrettably named Michigan Cool Cities initiative to Montgomery, Alabama's "Capital Cool," such projects prove that calling yourself cool is decidedly uncool. You can't chase cool. You can't court cool. You have to relax into cool. You fall into cool when you are comfortable enough in your own skin not to care what others think. Slogans and ad campaigns on this theme are easy to make but feel hollow. True authenticity and self-confidence is not easy but should be a goal for our communities.

In the spring of 2013, I was asked to be part of a local panel discussion titled "Tampa's Curious Quest To Be Cool." The other panelists and I all agreed how uncool it is to actually chase cool. I was searching for a good Tampa example of authenticity and self-confidence to share with the audience, and I found a great one in Tampa Mayor Bob Buckhorn.

I asked the audience for a show of hands if three years ago they thought Bob Buckhorn was cool. Not a single hand went up. I asked how many thought Bob Buckhorn was cool now, and over half the audience raised their hand. From zero to over 50% "cool approval" in less than three years is an example that others, both people and communities, would do well to emulate. But how did he do it?

Mayor Buckhorn has come a long way since his days as a city councilman dueling with local strip club owner Joe Redner over the infamous 'six foot' rule that prohibited dancers from getting too close to patrons; all in the name of health and safety. More recently, he went from an underdog mayoral candidate to becoming a truly effective and dynamic mayor. *The Tampa Bay Times* gave him outstanding grades at the halfway mark of his first term.[xliv]

Mayor Buckhorn is not a different man than he was a few years ago, but he has clearly found his niche, his perfect job, and his comfort zone. He now speaks passionately about Tampa and his desire to create a great city for his kids to return to after graduation from college. He is cool now because he has found his voice and is speaking from the heart—and it shows. If cool was just a different suit, a haircut or a clever talking point, cool would be easy. But that's not what cool is, and chasing cool by adopting such affectations is a losing proposition. A city becomes cool when it is authentic and honest about it its strengths and weaknesses, and when it stops comparing itself to others. Our relentless "benchmarking" with other cities serves a technical purpose, but it should not be the measure of our contentment with our own community. Bob Buckhorn found his authentic cool and his mojo by finding his authentic spot. By not trying to be cool, he has become cool.

Cool is, in economic terms, a "positional good." Coined by economist Fred Hirsch, the term positional good refers to products or services that derive value from their desirability in comparison with substitutes. Because this desirability comes from people's attitudes towards the respective goods and services, the value becomes highly subjective. So cool, while clearly very valuable, can also be incredibly ephemeral. If you are lucky enough to actually catch a cool spark, you should enjoy it while it lasts because, like youth, it can be all too fleeting.

In his 2002 book, *The Rise of the Creative Class*, Richard Florida relates a story about a student who was about to graduate from Carnegie Mellon University, where Florida was then a professor. The student had multiple job options but had selected Austin, Texas. When asked by Florida why he had chosen that city, the student eloquently replied, "Because it's Austin, man."

Austin had managed to capture something important and highly ephemeral. It had captured cool. It had captured the hearts and minds of the highly mobile, educated, creative workforce as *the* place to be. It had a global reputation for music, technology and film centered on the amazing SXSW conference. It was home to Dell, Whole Foods and the University of Texas. It was also the state capital of Texas.

Today Austin remains all of those things, but during a recent visit there I heard from many people who thought that Austin was "over" or had become "too Hollywood." Perhaps a victim of its own success, Austin has seen its cost of living increase, the gentrification of its cool neighborhoods, and a large influx of newcomers who seem to some to have diluted what made Austin unique and desirable to begin with.

In early 2013, I visited Denver, Colorado, and was amazed by the energy that the city exuded. Between 2002 and 2012, Denver's population grew at an average annual rate of 1.4%. Metro Denver has one of the nation's strongest metropolitan economies. Median household income in the area was $59,230 in 2011, compared to the national median income of $50,054. In 2012, it enjoyed 2.4% job growth and 3.3% economic growth.[xlv] The city is highly educated, with 40.5% of residents holding a bachelor's degree or higher. And it ranks first among large U.S. metropolitan areas for total population gain in the coveted 25- to 34-year age group between 2008 and 2010. Young, educated and creative people love Denver's combination of jobs, culture, food, beer, mass transit, natural environment and recreational activities.

People I spoke with in Denver were well aware of its growth and talked about the excitement they felt for the area. They talked in glowing terms about how much the city had changed in the past few years. And though many were relative newcomers to the area, they already felt plugged into the city.

I have been back to Denver several times since that 2013 visit, and I am continually impressed with the city. Denver now enjoys the type of reputation that Austin held ten years ago—and both Denver and Austin should be OK with that. Being the hot "it" city is a great thing, but it is not a lasting designation. I would liken it to being a popular movie star who is "having a moment." The experience is great while it lasts, but to have a long lasting career or to be a long-term great city you need to be focused on longevity. Build on current energy and excitement to lay the groundwork for the future. I certainly do not believe Austin is "over," but it clearly has shifted into its next phase of being. Let Denver carry the mantle of cool now and enjoy it while it lasts. The next "it" city is laying the groundwork even as we speak, and that is exciting.

RAISING EXPECTATIONS

There are risks that come along with bringing in new people and new ideas for communities. There is financial risk—minimal, I believe—and some political risk. Another new risk and fear for cities may be that of raised expectations. The glow of initial success will only last so long and usually begets the inevitable question of what's next. Success in the arena of emotional engagement will no doubt raise the hopes and expectations of citizens, which means that you have to continue to respond and improve in this area as a city-maker. It is like giving a great birthday gift to your spouse. They love it, and you feel great—until next year when the pressure to raise the bar sets in—not necessarily logical, but a real consideration nonetheless. If you let your actions be governed by this anxiety, you would never want to make a grand effort but instead dole out in small, blandly consistent increments the love that you feel for your spouse. Such an arrangement would be satisfying neither to the recipient nor the giver. When we do something special, we feel good. When we receive something special, we feel great. It is not just the receiver but also the giver who benefits.

Raised expectations should be seen as a good thing because when we take back our cities and become makers, we bear the risk and responsibility of being good caretakers of that community. We are essentially expecting more from ourselves and, in doing so, we push each other to rise to a new level of achievement and even exceed it. I know I said that we should "aim low" (in the first chapter), but that is in how to enter the game, not a limit on the scale of our hopes and dreams. The best citizenry will inspire the least engaged and challenge those in the middle to be just a little bit better than they were.

"Urban citizenship," a concept coined by Giorgio DiCicco, the author and former poet laureate of Toronto, explains this interconnected relationship. DiCicco notes that urban citizenship comes with higher stakes than plain citizenship because we live in closer proximity to each other. By choosing the urban option, we are opting into all the benefits: economic advantages, a higher level of opportunity for engagement, cultural enrichment and social interaction. These benefits also carry a responsibility as well; we must be patient and tolerant of others, we must follow societal norms and customs, and to truly reciprocate the blessings of urban citizenship we must be active participants in making the experience of our city.

I love DiCicco's thinking on this matter. He is challenging us. To be fully realized as a citizen, it is not enough merely to obey the law, pay your taxes and spend your money. We should start projects, volunteer, join a movement, make a gesture. Become something more than a consumer of your city, and you become part of the engine that moves the community forward. Raising our expectations of ourselves and each other may lead to some disappointments when we fail to meet those elevated standards, but it is in the trying that interesting, valuable and sometimes wonderful things happen.

TAKING THE PROBLEMATIC WITH THE GOOD

In opening the door to more citizen engagement, cities are inevitably going to run into circumstances where people don't follow every rule or tread into territory that official folks would have preferred was left alone. If we want the good and positive of community engagement, we need to be willing to take some of the challenges that will inevitably arise. Some will argue that by letting people into the process, the door is opening on potential anarchy—to which I reply that cities need to trust their citizens to do the right and needed thing. Citizens, for the most part, have incredible natural radars regarding where danger lies and how far is too far. Law professors and naysayers love to invoke the "slippery slope" as a way to deny action. But this idea implies that we, as citizens, do not have the common sense to intuit where our natural boundaries lay. It assumes the most dire and drastic end result when there is obvious middle ground. The genius of the community as a collective group, which possesses collective wisdom, is that it is really good at finding new equilibrium. Events may occur that upset that equilibrium, but communities need to trust that citizens can try something new and not lose their sense of balance and identity. In fact, jumping in and engaging a few times, especially on smaller projects, teaches us that we can quickly find new ground, not teeter over the edge, and become better community builders along the way.

Chapter Five
Remember...

WHO OWNS IT MATTERS

When it comes to changing how a city is perceived, who bears the new idea/concept matters. A lot. Message and messenger inevitably become tied together, and that person or organization becomes the "owner" of the message. Depending on the owner, we hear the message differently as the audience. When *Forbes* declares our city a Top 10 destination, we hear it differently than when our chamber of commerce says the same thing. When the mayor says our city is a great place to live, work and play—we hear it differently than when our buddy from college extols the same virtues of the community. The mayor and the chamber are supposed to be saying these things, so when they declare success, we think it's part of their pitch. What they are saying may well be true, but we don't feel the validity of their claims in the same way we do when the message comes from a third party or, better yet, a trusted friend. Something to keep in mind when crafting a new message or idea is that the person or source who carries the message or idea into the community becomes incredibly important. Sometimes that necessitates finding a better "owner" to move the message forward, which is what happened in Muskegon, Michigan.

In June 2011, I spoke in Muskegon at the invitation of their Community Foundation and Chamber of Commerce. My partner Michelle Royal and I also delivered one of my first community workshops there—For the Love of Muskegon—which brought out nearly 100 citizens to generate energy and ideas about how to better love the community. In the months that followed, I would receive periodic updates from our new friends there. It seemed like good things grew out of the engagement, especially from the Community Foundation, which instigated a micro-grant program after seeing how excited people became about the $500 idea challenge and how impactful small amounts of money could be in the hands of people who loved their city. Then, toward the end of the year, something small and unintended emerged from that place of community love.

In late 2011, New Belgium Brewery, a successful microbrewery from Colorado had put out the word that they were looking for new places to expand their operations. Via social media, they challenged communities to show the company why their city was a great place for New Belgium to consider. A group of young professionals from Muskegon, being both beer lovers and city lovers, thought a new brewery would be a great addition to the community. They decided to stage a group photo in Lake Michigan that would show how much they loved their city. On a very cold December day, these thirteen people stripped down to swimsuits and waded into chilly Lake Michigan carrying letters that spelled out "LOVE MUSKEGON." And they shot this photo:

Photo courtesy of Mark Gongalski

The photo hit social media and immediately raced through the online community—not just in Muskegon but around the state. Local media picked it up and published several stories about the performance. People were talking about how much those folks in Muskegon must love their community, not realizing that it was also a stunt to get better beer. The publicity stunt aspect did not matter; the photo became a real tipping point and catalyst for the community.

The Community Foundation and Chamber of Commerce, the organizations that originally brought me to Muskegon, realized that the image and excitement surrounding it presented an important opportunity. "Love Muskegon" could be a great boost for the area, and they wanted to make sure the slogan would stick. But they very wisely realized that if they were to lead the campaign, then Love Muskegon would become a phenomenon associated with the marketing efforts of the foundation and chamber—they would "own" it. The leaders of both organizations quietly convened several participants from the photo shoot, which included young professional leaders and, luckily, some creative staffers from a local ad agency. Chamber and foundation representatives told the makers of the original photo that they loved the concept and wanted to support it, but they did not want to be seen as the entities backing it. They wanted these young leaders to take up the mantle and be the standard bearers of the campaign. The foundation and the chamber would put money into the idea but wanted to be able to publicly deny active involvement. This suited the young leaders of the newfound group just fine.

With a little bit of financial support, they were able to commission a fantastic logo and begin to circulate the image and message out into the community. Love Muskegon was born. The project would be open-sourced and accessible to all. The group behind the slogan posted logo files online and invited anyone to use them and come up with new ideas. Publicly, the foundation and chamber applauded the new-found enthusiasm and found official ways to work with this new organization. Over the next year, the logo would appear all over the city, including hand-drawn versions inscribed on windshields and chalked on sidewalks. Love Muskegon events proliferated—from block parties to art openings to meet-ups. The city found an innovative way to support the movement by agreeing to waive event permit fees for any Love Muskegon event. By doing this, they brilliantly encouraged events to become part of the broader campaign.

The movement took on some strange and wonderful aspects as well. In early 2012, "green people" started to appear at events throughout the city. Clad from head to toe in bright green body stockings, these anonymous love ambassadors would show up wearing Love Muskegon clothing while handing out Love Muskegon swag and information. To me, this shows how wonderfully creative a community can be if they are primed and encouraged. I think it unlikely that an official organiza-tion like a chamber of commerce would have come up with the idea of the green people, but the creative community of Muskegon—those who love their city—did come up with this crazy, wonderful manifestation of love.

John Howkins is the author of *The Creative Economy*, and along with Charles Landry and Richard Florida, a true glob-al thinker on creativity and cities. He pointed out to me that "interesting places are interesting usually because of the actions of private individuals, not governments." He suggested that the growth of government-led initiatives is founded on a misguided notion that governments run cities. He is certainly correct that when the officials own something, it feels different. I am sure that if the chamber or city had overtly led the Love Muskegon campaign, it would have been a success. Their community was ready for the idea. But because Love Muskegon was an open-source, grassroots effort, it engaged multiple tiers of people as owners of the project. These individuals became leaders, owners and champions instead of standing on the sidelines and applauding.

Realizing that they had limited resources and hoping something cool would happen, the leadership in Muskegon rolled the dice—and enabled something wonderful. Doing so was clearly a risk for official city makers and one I applaud them for taking. They did not get to take the credit, but they also shielded from some of the risk of failure. They also don't carry the burden of ongoing maintenance and upkeep of the projects associated with Love Muskegon. This position represents a third option between the standard choices of government-led or private sector-led projects: government acting as deal-maker, as venture capitalist and matchmaker of people and ideas. We don't usually think of our governments as being so artful and deft, but they clearly can be if they are not politicking to see who gets the credit or who takes the blame. Such restraint can be a tall order in our highly partisan times, but I am continually encouraged by the local politicians I meet who have a passion for their places that cuts across party ideologies. Local leaders are about getting things done, and the best of them know that a win for the community translates into a win for them as well.

SUPPORT YOUR HIGH TOUCH ENTREPRENEURS

Nearly every city talks a good game about entrepreneurs. Most cities wants more entrepreneurs and are trying to cultivate a more entrepreneurial culture. That's great. But I get the sense that when cities and chambers of commerce are talking about entrepreneurs, they are talking about high tech entrepreneurs. Those sleek tech, mobile computing, app-developing folks that may create the next Facebook, Google or Angry Birds. We would love to have such people and such companies in our communities. The reality is that tech attracts tech. Communities where an established tech industry already exists have so many advantages in this area that it is very hard for other communities to gain a foothold.

In 2011, one of Tampa's emerging tech stars, a company named Wufoo, was purchased by Survey Monkey, a Silicon Valley based company. Many cheered—one of our locally grown companies had broken through and was on the national tech map. By extension, people felt, Tampa was now on the map as well. Sadly, one of the conditions of the purchase was that the whole Wufoo team of ten people had to move to California. This is the reality of growing a local tech industry; the most successful emerging ventures are very likely to be noticed and pulled into the orbit of giants such as Silicon Valley, New York City or North Carolina's Research Triangle. That does not mean we should stop emphasizing our local tech scene—far from it. High tech entrepreneurs create an environment of excitement and energy that everyone can benefit from. They open up our eyes to the possibilities of technology, and they keep us thinking about the future. We just need to be aware of the realities of the industry. Like a town that exports its best and brightest to outside colleges and universities never to see those kids return, tech talent drain is a very real possibility.

When it comes to entrepreneurs, I also get the sense from cities that they are talking about high employment entrepreneurs. These are the businesses that will employ hundreds, maybe even thousands of people. They are the kind of business that check off multiple boxes on the economic development scorecard. Bagging an "elephant" is great when it happens, but such opportunities require a rare combination of assets, timing, luck and patience. Because high employment companies are so valuable, they often receive the lion's share of attention and resources, even if most of them don't pan out. I'm not suggesting that we stop trying to hit a home run, but our preoccupation with large companies can have a dampening affect on the local small business community. Smaller local businesses see all the love large corporations collect in the form of tax incentives, land deals, and general sucking up—and they ask "what about us?"

I believe we need to start paying more attention to the "high touch" entrepreneurs in our communities. These are the entrepreneurs who create the wonderful businesses that make our places feel special and our cities feel like home. Think about your favorite local restaurant or the coffee shop where you meet friends to hang out (or write books!). How about your favorite food truck or the game store where you play Magic the Gathering or Dungeons & Dragons? These businesses will not employ hundreds of people or have an IPO. In fact, they may only employ a handful of people and make a nominal impact in pure economic terms. But we all know these types of places make our communities special.

In *For the Love of Cities*, I profiled Detroit co-creator Phil Cooley. Phil and his friends rehabbed an old building in the Corktown neighborhood of Detroit and opened up Slow's BBQ, one of the hottest restaurants in the city. The restaurant became a beacon for other entrepreneurs, who in turn began to regard Corktown as a place ready for renewal. Since Slow's broke the ice, many more businesses, especially restaurants, have come back to the neighborhood. In fact, in 2012, Bon Appetit magazine named Corktown "Detroit's Coolest Nabe"[1] (that's hipster for neighborhood). Phil has gone on to open up a B&B and become part of a 100,000-sq-foot business and arts accelerator called Pony Ride.

Phil has grown into a kind of rock star social entrepreneur, someone who the political and economic leadership of Detroit lavishes with lots of (well-deserved) attention. At heart, he is the classic high touch entrepreneur. His businesses are about people and great experiences, not about profit maximization. Until he started receiving media attention from local publications like *Model D*, and then national publications like *The New York Times*, he was just a restaurant owner to the city. People began to realize that his business had become an anchor and a bright spot that others were rallying around. Suddenly, they were paying attention.

Part of the challenge for cities and the traditional business community in dealing with Phil is that he is not your classic entrepreneur; mostly because he does not seem to be motivated by the traditional driver of profit. So the traditional economic development levers are less effective with him. Folks like Phil don't usually show up on the radar of the economic development teams because on the economic development scorecard, high touch entrepreneurs don't score many points. That is why such a scorecard cannot be the ultimate guide for our economic development policies.

High touch businesses may not carry much economic weight, but they carry lots of psychic and emotional significance. When a business like Slow's dares to defy logic and prevailing economic thinking by going into a distressed neighborhood, such as Corktown was several years ago, it can change the trajectory of the community. The beloved business becomes a catalyst for reinvention because someone—an entrepreneur, defined as "one who notices opportunity"—is willing to take a chance. These are the types of businesses that simply make us feel good. They need to be valued for that in our economic scorecard. My hope is that we can change our thinking and recognize high touch entrepreneurs as a key part of a healthy, diverse community ecosystem.

Liz Lessner is a restaurateur from Columbus, Ohio. She opened her first restaurant in Columbus in 2001 and now runs a Columbus Food League that consists of six "fiercely independent, anti-establishment" restaurants. She has also become the de facto leader of a group of downtown Columbus-based social entrepreneurs who are trying to improve the city while making a profit. She seeks out locations that are informed in part on emerging community needs and in doing so, much like Phil Cooley, creates a restaurant that is also a signal that the neighborhood is ready for change.

While Cooley is quiet to the point of seeming shy, Lessner is an exuberant personality who is known for speaking up. She has become a master at engaging media, both traditional and social, to bring attention to her causes. "I'm a good advocate and agitator—at forming collaborations, getting things done," she says.

I asked Lessner about her reputation, and she acknowledged that sometimes a fight is necessary. "My role is to be the loud business owner," she told me over coffee in the Short North neighborhood of Columbus. Lessner is not one to let her small economic size diminish her voice. She has recognized that even a small business owner can shape the conversation in a city, if she decides to do so. I believe Columbus listens to Lessner in no small part because her businesses are very high touch. They are establishments that thousands of citizens know and love.

Others may not draw the media attention that Cooley and Lessner do, but their presence is critical to community success. In Cedar Rapids, a city that is rebuilding from the floods of 2009, small business openings or re-openings are seen as milestones, especially in neighborhoods that were hard hit. New Bo Books is in the New Bohemia neighborhood of Cedar Rapids. The neighborhood is coming back strong and even better than it was before. A new city market, a beach volleyball park and other small businesses showcase a vitality that is drawing many into the area.

Mary Ann Peters opened the bookstore in the summer of 2012 in partnership with the famous Prairie Lights Bookstore in Iowa City. New Bo has become the place in Cedar Rapids where people meet and talk about the community. Be it through a book signing, a book club or just people dropping by to chat, the bookstore, like hundreds of other independent bookstores across the country, provides a psychic anchor far more valuable than the store's size would imply. New Bo Books is small – very small—but it has heart and a good story. Peters not only opened the business, she lives just a block away. The bookstore will never employ many people, but it signifies progress and hope to an area of town that some thought would never come back. Such high touch entrepreneurs need to be recognized for the impact they have, far beyond pure economics, for making great neighborhoods and places that we love. Most of them operate under the official radar, and they seem fine with that. Imagine what impact they might have if they received just a sliver of the love that we give large or high tech businesses.

PLAY AT YOUR OWN LEVEL

I routinely hear from communities about their desire to involve affluent citizens more deeply. Most communities already have a group of go-to leaders with deep pockets who they routinely tap for projects. To their credit, these leaders, let's call them "whales," often step up and support whatever is asked of them. Early on in my business career, I got to know one of the most prominent Tampa Bay whales, a gentleman named Ray Murray. By the time I met Ray, he had been retired for many years, having sold his main company for many millions of dollars. Like most entrepreneurs, he liked being around business, so he still kept an office, a CFO and enough little investments to keep him busy. He said he had no interest in playing golf. (In fact, he once gave me his slot at the local Senior PGA pro-am. Thanks again, Ray!) His office was in the same building as mine, and I could see a constant stream of people coming in to visit him. He and his wife were generous supporters of the arts, and he became the main patron of the Florida Orchestra.

Every community has a leader like Ray, probably many of them. When people like Ray get involved in their community, buildings get built, endowments are created, and hospitals add wings. Of course communities want more of their affluent constituents into the game—they bring so much potential to the table. The city process of "whale hunting" typically involves the local community foundation, the chamber of commerce leadership, mayors and city council. It is a long, slow process of building relationships and finding the right opportunity to engage.

People need to be allowed to enter the game at their own level. Ray Murray is not likely to volunteer to man the water station at the local Susan G. Komen 5K. But others who don't have the same financial resources will want to give their time and talents in those ways. The notion to give, be it in big or small ways, is the heart of engagement. It needs to be nurtured and cultivated over time to turn young professionals and recent graduates into esteemed community elders who can literally shift a community's fortunes with their efforts.

We need to remember that people, no matter their economic status, are moved by a desire to do something for their community that is, at its core, the same from person to person: the desire to make meaning and to make some aspect of a community better. The latter drive often falls into the category of enlightened self-interest, if the part of the community that is the target of philanthropy is also where the philanthropist lives or spends time. If we make our immediate community better, we are making our own lives better. Ray Murray's support for the Florida Orchestra had some self-interest in it—he is a huge fan of classical music, and while he did not want his community to be without this cultural amenity, he also wanted to hear his Mozart and Beethoven.

I wrote at length about our desire to make meaning in *For the Love of Cities*. It remains a recurring theme and motivation that I see in communities all over the world. Those who would step up and do something above and beyond ordinary citizenship do so not out of financial motivation, but out of a desire to create, to put an imprint on something and say, "I made that." Small or large, "I made that" is a powerful motivator and a deeply satisfying reward.

GO DEEPER

In *For the Love of Cities* I talked about the "amenities game" that nearly every city plays. It is the standard way of promoting and "selling" your city. You list all of your great amenities, from professional sports to performing arts centers to quality healthcare, and you invite people (and businesses) to come and partake of your bounty. This approach is all well and good, but the amenities game privileges larger places, which will always beat smaller places in this particular game. I cautioned smaller cities about playing this game and suggested that such places look at opportunities to maximize meaning, as well as amenities, as a possible way to engage more purpose-driven co-creators and citizens. The ability to make a difference in your community can be a powerful lure and an anchor that keeps your most engaged citizens in your city. In smaller places, we can see the impact of our efforts, and such feedback is immensely important to our sense of accomplishment.

Another potential pitfall for smaller cities, similar to the amenities game, is the understandable inclination to go wide, to try to expand the scope of offerings and amenities. For example—trying to add more restaurants. Growing the number of restaurants in your city is fine but unlikely to yield the significant results hoped for. Two more restaurants in a town of 30,000 is not going to make you Chicago. It would be nice to have the additional options but probably not a significant gain. At best, the restaurants might become an exceptional icon that differentiates the city, a world-class, five-star Alice Waters-type experience in an unexpected place. That could be a game changer for the city's identity. At worst, the addition is poorly executed, and people lament that they can't get good whatever in your town. More likely it would pan out to be something in between: a nice restaurant where people can say "this is as good as we get in Chicago." And there is the problem. Many times the addition, this process of going wide, actually underscores the advantage that the larger city already has. It feels like a backhanded compliment that is meant to remind you that you are small and the other place is bigger and better.

Worse still is the strategy of attracting a recognized chain restaurant to your smaller community. "We got an Olive Garden" may be seen as a win in traditional economic development terms (new jobs, new business, grand opening, etc.), but that Olive Garden does nothing to distinguish your city. Chains are predicated upon predictability and consistency from location to location. This is not to knock Olive Garden (I do love their breadsticks), but their arrival homogenizes your community, which diminishes one of the advantages smaller communities have—their local charm.

What if your small town focused instead on going deep? To dig into the very elements which distinguish it from larger places in first place. This requires us to admit that we are not, nor will we ever be, the larger city that small places inevitably measure themselves against.

In 2012, I was in a small beach town in Northern New Zealand called Tutukaka, a resort town where about 1,200 full-time residents live. During the summer, the population can fluctuate to over 4,000 with many seasonal visitors arriving on their yachts. During those months, the main hotel and restaurants are full, and the dive and fishing boats are very busy. In the off-season, the place is very quiet and mostly empty. Tutukaka does not need another restaurant or more retail. That would not sustain the town or improve quality of life in the community. What the community needs to do is look at the very elements that make it special. The obvious ones are water, beaches, boats and diving. But how about digging deeper into some other characteristics, such as the quiet, pitch-black nights that offer amazing stargazing or the empty beaches? Yes, empty beaches.

My friend Grant Tromp rides his bike in Tutukaka, and he noticed that when he rides on the beaches in the early mornings, his wheels create an almost artistic design in the sand. He began a project to recruit other cyclists to join him in creating sand art, mostly for their own amusement. Grant has taken a negative factor (empty beaches) and transformed it into something that is at least interesting and, potentially, a boon to the community.

Photo courtesy of Grant Tromp

What if Tutukaka's leaders were to go deeper into this idea of empty beaches and allow bonfires in winter or camping on the beaches during the off-season? Perhaps not every night but one weekend a month or the like could help bring in off-season adventurers seeking a unique experience. Even locals might like to experience a fire or a chance to sleep under the stars on a beautiful and quiet New Zealand beach.

Going deep means looking at the native characteristics of your community and thinking about them in a different way. From this perspective, traditional weaknesses become potential opportunities and quirky, local color becomes the basis for new experiences. Another great example actually comes from Grant's wife, Brigitte Legendre. A passionate roller skater, Brigitte decided to share her love for the sport and created Tutukaka's first roller disco night in early 2012. It proved very popular, and the town now hosts multiple events each month including roller derby and roller disco. People have created a skate culture in the region. Who would have imagined that roller skating and Tutukaka would go together except someone like Brigitte, whose innate characteristics provided an opportunity for her community to go deeper?

Merrill, Wisconsin, is a small town of 9,600 just north of Wausau in central Wisconsin and, as they say, "the gateway to the north woods." In April 2011, the town was hit by an E3 tornado that caused considerable damage to its industrial park, some homes and city fairgrounds. Remarkably, no one was killed, but the longstanding bleachers at the fairgrounds did not fare so well. In 2013, the city had an opportunity to rebuild with funds from insurance. Instead of just rebuilding the stands, they proposed to build an enclosed expo center, which would cost several times more than replacing the outdoor stands. The primary reason they wanted to proceed with an enclosed space was that, over the years, Merrill had become home to one of North America's best rodeos.

Named the nation's best small rodeo several times and a hugely popular regional tradition, the Merrill Rodeo had outgrown the capacity of the old fairgrounds. The tornado actually created an opportunity for the town to grow, expand and leverage a truly unique local asset. The rodeo organizers had told the city that with an enclosed facility they could host multiple rodeo events, including their own. The other events would be lured there because of the reputation and expertise of the Merrill rodeo.

The project remains stuck in discussions between the city and county as to how best to proceed with redevelopment. The rodeo, to their credit, has remained in Merrill even though the lack of any grandstand has forced them to rent bleachers since the tornado. A feasibility study is underway that includes transfer of ownership from the county to the city and, at the very least, a new grandstand has been promised by 2015 or 2016.[xlvi]

Just north of Merrill sits the town of Tomahawk, Wisconsin. The town of 3,500 residents is also home to a large Harley Davidson parts manufacturing facility. Because of this, motorcycles, especially Harleys, are a key part of local identity. The city's signature event is an annual Fall Ride where Harley owners from all over North America descend on Tomahawk in a mini Sturgis Rally-type event. The town swells to over 20,000 visitors during that week.

These three small communities have gone deeper into their own identity to find authentic elements from which they have built successful projects. For cities such as Tomahawk, the key piece is pretty obvious. For cities such as Merrill, the key piece grows over time and may not have been obvious at first. And for cities like Tutukaka, the key piece must be searched for, because it is far from obvious and, in fact, may need to be teased out of the people who live there. Every place, big or small, has amazing, creative people and unique opportunities, which can become anchors for something wonderful for the community. We just need to take the time and make the effort to look deeper to see them.

EMBRACE THE MULTI-SENSORY LANDSCAPE OF CITIES

In his 2012 book, *The Sensory Landscape of Cities*, Charles Landry dissects how we, as human beings in cities, experience those cities through our multiple senses. He calls the city a "360 degree enveloping, immersive experience which has emotional and psychological impacts" but one that we are, sadly, taking in via "increasingly narrow funnels of perception."[1] Though we have five senses, our thinking and practice around our cities has muted all these senses to the point that we are, like The Who's Tommy, deaf, dumb and blind to the vast experience of our places. Much of this shutting off is self-imposed. We isolate ourselves in our cars, or we tune out our world with our ear buds to the point where we could walk past a burning building with barely a second glance. At 45 mph, it is difficult to notice much more than the cars in front of you, let alone something small and subtle. In that environment of "impoverished awareness"[1] as Landry calls it, it's little wonder that we have become fixated on the few things that can break through and get our attention. The skyscraper, the professional sports stadium, the massive amenity and public artwork have become the favored tools of development because they are the only things that seem to register with our citizens. If we want to be able to experience our cities more fully, we will need to slow down the cars, encourage more density of human interaction, and re-prioritize the way we think about our cities.

Right now, most city planning seems to be in service to cars; where to park them, how to get them from point A to point B faster, how many can go here or there. We have privileged the car at the expense of the pedestrian and the cyclist, and we need to rebalance our accounting in order to improve the experience of our cities. We are missing out on great stuff. Every day we race past amazing feats of engineering, beautiful works of art and a cornucopia of interesting shops and restaurants without a second glance. As Landry says, our view of our cities is becoming increasingly narrow. The only way to change this state of affairs is to become intentional about getting out of our cars, walking more, exploring and discovering our places. Once we do so, we open up our other senses and enrich the experience of our places.

Most of the time, we don't realize what we are missing because we have become overly dependent on the visual inputs of our places. Clearly how a place looks is incredibly important, but I believe we have great opportunities to make our places surprising and delightful if we think about tapping into our other senses.

I was in San Luis Obispo, California, in early 2013. I had driven down the city's main downtown road, Higuera Street. It is a stunningly beautiful street with the most amazing tree canopy I have ever seen in a city. While driving, this canopy is the most obvious and memorable aspect of the downtown. But later, as I was walking down Higuera Street, I smelled an amazing combination of chocolates and sweets, which led me into a lovely candy store. On a warm evening, it offered an intoxicating smell and a great place for an after-dinner nibble—one that I literally found by following my nose.

In Greenville, South Carolina, I had a similar experience as I walked their lovely Main Street. At the corner of Main and McBee, the city has put dozens of bells in the trees. When a breeze blows, the bells create a wind chime effect that is distinct to that particular street corner. I asked local author and journalist John Boyanoski about the bells, and he said that the city had purchased them years ago at a home improvement store and hung them up. The city had planned to do so all along Main Street, but in the end only did it at one intersection. I love this. It was very cheap and easy to implement. It is a simple love note that will surprise and delight visitors and locals alike. And it is one that can only be experienced by opening up more of our senses and taking in the broader landscape.

Our cities are speaking to us across multiple channels. They are multifaceted puzzles that invite exploration and play. We have fixated on one or two of these channels, but if we just opened ourselves to other possibilities we would see that there are many simple and inexpensive opportunities to engage people.

BE BETTER STORYTELLERS

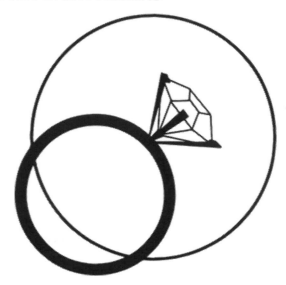

Today cities have more media outlets and opportunities than ever before. From a highly segmented and voracious print and television market, to an exponentially increasing number of social media platforms, we have more avenues for communication than ever before and at speeds that can give you whiplash faster than you can say "Justine Sacco." For better or worse, a tweet can change the direction of your life or your city. Just ask Justine Sacco. For those who don't recognize the name, she was the PR "professional" who posted a racist tweet in late 2013 before boarding a plane to South Africa. By the time she had landed, the tweet had gone viral; there were thousands of condemnations across the Internet, and she had been fired by her agency. It can happen that fast.

Along with the power to disseminate information at unprecedented speeds, we are generating mountains of data about our cities, much of it in real time. These facts and figures document every aspect of our communities and our lives in them. We use these data points all the time to make the case for the excellence of our cities. "Crime rate drops 5%" or "downtown occupancy rates at 98%" are typical examples of the data we use to promote our places. But most people don't remember facts and figures; they remember good stories. Instead of giving me data about why your city is great, tell me a story that makes me believe your city is great.

Greg Burris, the city manager from Springfield, Missouri, who I mentioned in Chapter One, related a story to me about the importance of being better storytellers. Early in his tenure as city manager, Burris was in one of the regular meetings he had with the city's department heads. He overheard the public works staff talking about something interesting that had happened that week. A woman had called the city in a panic because her elderly mother, who suffered from dementia, had apparently flushed her jewelry, including her wedding ring down the toilet. The family could not find the jewelry and wanted to know if the public works department, which manages the sewer system, could help. They researched her neighborhood and found the schematic for the area. They sent a robot into the sewers to check a catch basin and, sure enough. they found the jewelry and the precious ring. The family was ecstatic. Burris said he about jumped out of his chair asking the public works guys why they had not made a big deal about this. They said they were just doing their job and not looking for applause. He told his department leaders that this was not about taking a bow, but rather showing the community that their city works. All the data in the world is not worth a great story like the public works department finding this woman's wedding ring. People would remember that story and feel better about their city because of it. Every day cities do amazing things. If citizens only knew about them, they would say "wow" or "thank you." By becoming better storytellers, we can build up the confidence of our citizens in our cities and counteract the daily barrage of negative stories that traditional media pumps out.

Burris made sure that each department had the authority to tell stories via social media and through the city's communications team. He didn't just empower them, he challenged them to find and tell a better story. Social media has given us more outlets for all of our data, but more information does not beget better storytelling. In addition to providing technology and media training, we should also be providing training in how to be better storytellers. Does your city or department have a chief storyteller? Stories have an arc—a beginning, a middle conflict and an end. They have heroes, they have villains, and they have challenges that are overcome. They have heart. A press release is not a story. But behind the press release, buried in the facts and figures, there may be an interesting story that needs to be told.

Some will say that the brevity of social media does not lend itself to storytelling, but I like to think of this as a creative challenge. Remember the famous short story often attributed to Ernest Hemmingway: "For sale: baby shoes, never worn." Heartbreaking, and it even could have fit into a 140-character tweet! So a Vine can be a 6-second movie, Instagram a postcard, and by comparison your Facebook page can practically be a novel. Tell better stories with your data—people will remember you, the story and maybe even the data.

ACTIVATE YOUR COMMUNITY

Activate is an interesting word. It is not the same as "start," "launch" or even "begin." All of the latter words imply a more focused effort, perhaps even a Herculean one, on the part of someone to make something happen. Think about launch. Many of us imagine a rocket and that explosive moment of inception, followed by a river of jet fire that hurls the rocket skyward. A launch is an exciting moment because of its grand spectacle, display of power and potential danger. People come out to watch a rocket launch. They also come out to watch a rocket landing, be it a space shuttle touchdown or an ocean splashdown. But in between the actual work occurs, and it is often less interesting to the broad public. We like the explosive beginning and the triumphant end—the middle part, less so. This attitude carries over to our community efforts as well.

We love the big project, the grand effort and the ribbon cutting for the completed goal. But such projects require time, focused effort and in many cases, lots and lots of resources. Our leaders get fixated on such big projects, and our fellow citizens have come to believe that city making is defined by these signature projects. We have lost the sense that small efforts, *our* small efforts as citizens, can make a difference. The co-creators and community activists in our midst know this, but we need to convince more of our friends and neighbors, that they, too, play a part in the process.

We need to learn to appreciate the concept of activate. Unlike start or launch, activate feels different. Activate feels chemical. It speaks to the stored potential of various elements and hints at their capacity to do something if brought together and catalyzed. Think of the science projects we did as kids when we combined baking soda with vinegar to create a "volcano" for science class. Who knew that we could make that happen simply by bringing those elements into contact with each other? Activate feels less about control or focused effort and more about allowing potential, the stored energy of people, to come forth and manifest in their community. Our leaders have finite time and resources, which means a limited number of starts and launches, a limited amount of anything that requires oversight and control. But our leaders have far greater ability to play the alchemist and try to encourage various elements to accidentally-intentionally come into contact with each other and perhaps spark something. "Activate" requires patience and a willingness to experiment. When two elements don't mix in the way you anticipated and you burn your eyebrows off, you learn an important lesson. When seemingly compatible and synergistic elements don't coalesce into something and just remain inert, we need to note that failure to launch and move on. When you are able to bring elements together and they click, and maybe even do something totally amazing and unexpected, that is the metaphorical moment of turning lead into gold.

What you are searching for is the community equivalent of a bottle of Diet Coke and a Mento. Nearly everyone has seen a YouTube video of people making fountains or rockets from ordinary two-liter bottles of Diet Coke by simply dropping one Mento into the bottle. (If you haven't seen this trick, do not try it at home! Go to YouTube and check out a video.)

These are two cheap and common items. But when they come together, something amazing happens—they release the stored energy in each other with explosive results. Think about the first time someone accidentally dropped a Mento into their Coke. That must have been a "Holy $h#t" moment! Who would have imagined that two such innocuous things could be so amazing together. The idea went viral several years ago, and thousands of people posted videos of their experiments. As the concept matured, an interesting thing happened; people started to get really creative. They choreographed intricate shows like the Bellagio Fountains and used Coke bottles like rockets to propel other experiments. They took the original idea and built on it in amazing ways, engaging in exactly the kind of exponential value creation you hope will come about when you activate the various elements in your community.

We need to embrace the idea of activating our communities. Activation means we are looking to tap into the abilities and stored potential of our places and allow them to bloom. It means we are relinquishing some control in favor of the exponential opportunities that might follow. It means we believe in our citizens and trust them enough to become part of the mix. It means we are treating them like partners and participants in the community-making process and not just as customers and consumers of our city.

A final thought on experimentation. You will never have your Diet Coke-and-Mentos moment if you are controlling and prescriptive about who does what and how resources are supposed to be used. Government leaders struggle with the prospect of experimentation because it is easy for outside critics to second-guess such an effort and throw stones at it. "Why are we wasting the public's money on..." is a refrain that politicians hate to hear. It puts them on the defensive and sadly makes for a juicy story that the local media, ever hungry for the latest controversy, is happy to trumpet.

Albert Einstein said "A person who never made a mistake never tried anything new." Our leaders should proudly defend their experiments and their competent failures. If you do everything right, do the preparation and legwork, and something still fails, that should be okay. You learn a lot from that failure and move on. The business community, especially the tech community, knows this. If you don't do your homework and preparatory work, you don't put in the effort, you should be sacked. But competent experimentation should be applauded. It means we are stretching, we are thinking, and we are taking some risks. It means we are looking for the opportunity to make something better—maybe even amazing. Our leaders should stand by their record of experiments as well as their list of accomplishments, because each experiment, be it a launch or a fizzle, is an accomplishment.

In Conclusion: What's Next?

By this point you should be asking yourself "who is minding the emotional side of my city?" Who is the Chief Love Officer in my community? I believe that to be competitive, let alone successful, we must be intentional about the emotional well-being and engagement of our citizens. The best city leaders have long intuited this, and more and more smart city leaders have begun to recognize this fact. Such officials are at the early stages of making feeling part of the standard dialog and mechanics of city making. My advice to leaders, both official and unofficial, is to find someone whose job it is to care. You can add emotional engagement to the list of responsibilities for your staff (and you should), but it won't become a priority or part of their process until someone is beating the drum on the issue. Recall how most initial corporate and municipal forays into green and sustainability issues went: lots of talk, proclamations, memos, etc. But it was not until organizations hired their first "green" officer or employee to lead the effort that practices actually began to change.

So will it go with emotional engagement. It would be great if you called this person your "Chief Love Officer," though skeptics would probably have a field day with the title. Perhaps instead the duties are encompassed by "place making" or "citizen engagement" or "civic innovation." Situating this person in a particular department may prove challenging, because if you make this part of economic development or neighborhoods you have pigeonholed them to the rest of your departments. The function has to be one that cuts across departmental silos and, most importantly, across previously held beliefs about the role the city plays in citizen engagement. That may prove to be your toughest challenge. Your veteran city makers may struggle with this approach because they have a long-standing stake in how things are currently done. The emotional caretaker will need to sensitive and patient with internal staff while also looking towards new ways to engage the city. Everything needs to be on the table. They will need to see every community touch point as an opportunity to improve the relationship the city has with the citizen. They will need to look for opportunities to receive citizens' love and affection for the city, and the unfamiliar ways this may manifest. So, too, will they bear the occasional ire and disappointment of citizens when things don't go according to plan. Their goals should include enabling surprise and delight as well as lots of fun within the city. They need to be storytellers, but they also need to be listeners. Relationships are built on communication and the fundamental ability to hear what others are saying, thinking and feeling. Their day-to-day job needs to be minding relationships and doing the myriad small things and occasional big thing that engages our citizens emotionally.

This is a "service design" opportunity, but it goes beyond that. In addition to rethinking the way the city provides all its services and resources to the citizens, you need to look at all the ways the city can receive from the citizenry. Relationships are two-way streets, and if the city can think of itself as the recipient of time, energy and even love it will transform the current one-way pattern into something more equitable, more sustaining and ultimately more satisfying for everyone.

CODA

When we make our places better, we make ourselves better. Our place is the crucible in which we occur. In the past, we have thought that our existence with our cities, while connected at certain points, was largely external to who we were. It is easier and convenient to see a separation because we have compartmentalized the relationship into something that is merely functional and transactional. We obey the law, pay our taxes and spend our money. In return, the city provides the necessary infrastructure to support our existence: everything from roads and bridges, to police and fire service, to the regular collection of garbage at our curbside. In truth, the city provides much more, most of which is taken for granted by both the city and the citizen. In this sense,

I liken us to children living in our parents' home. We see them as authority figures, providers of food and shelter and, of course, we appreciated the gifts, vacations and other special things they gave us. But as children we did not fully appreciate the totality of what they provided us. (I know I did not). As children we chafed at the limits they placed on us ("11 p.m. curfew? But Dad..."), we bitched about our allowances and neglected our chores. It is only now, as adults and perhaps as parents ourselves, we see all that goes into creating and maintaining that environment. The sacrifices, the hard choices and having to deal with us – they probably deserved a medal for the efforts!

Today, we as citizens in our places need to grow up. We need to move beyond the parent/child relationship we have had with our places, and take our places as adults at the table. We are full, participatory partners in the process of city making. While there is no equality of power in this relationship, there is required an equality of caring. We are capable of doing extraordinary things to make our neighborhoods and even our entire cities better when we care to do so. We can be makers and co-creators of the content that is our community. The first step is the mature realization that we can, and should, play a part in the process.

And our cities need to stop thinking of us all as children. If you see yourself as parent, then children are your responsibility. If we see children as adults, we treat them differently and have different expectations. Certainly there will always be members of our community who, like children, must be protected, guided and nurtured. Some will need to be disciplined and even punished. But city leadership needs to find the space for those "adult children" who step up and want to become part of the solution for their places. Cities need them, and they want to be part of the mix. The only thing standing in the way is the long held procedural belief that city making is an official job—a belief that most citizens have as well!

It is said the heart draws poor boundaries, and thank goodness for that. We do not put boundaries or limits on our love of our family and friends, so let us not limit or compartmentalize our feelings for our community, either. Love and emotional engagement are too powerful as tools to not include in our city making kit. Emotions will take us all into extraordinary places that logic, sense and reason alone cannot and will not reach, but only if we allow for the possibility of putting them to work.

Postscript

Unlike my first book, this work was composed over several distinct writing sessions over an eighteen-month period. Here are several updates that I include here for your edification.

In July 2014, LeBron James announced his return to Cleveland to much rejoicing in Northeast Ohio and across the country. The nearly unanimously positive reaction to the story was almost the mirror opposite of the reaction to his 2010 decision to leave Cleveland for Miami. This is because the 2010 choice scared most cities and the 2014 choice brings hope to most cities.

In *For the Love of Cities* I wrote this about James leaving Northeast Ohio:

> *His decision broke the hearts of Cleveland sports fans and angered many around the country (about the only ones not disheartened by the move were the folks in Miami). People reacted negatively to James' departure because we all want our home teams and hometowns to succeed, and his leaving of Cleveland left an ache that many cities have felt as they lose their local talent to star cities. James will likely win championships in Miami, but I suspect they will not be as meaningful to him or to Miami as even a single championship would have meant to Cleveland.*

In his July 2014 letter announcing his return, James wrote this:

> *Our city hasn't had that feeling in a long, long, long time. My goal is still to win as many titles as possible, no question. But what's most important for me is bringing one trophy back to Northeast Ohio.*

James teaches cities an important lesson about their talent. When talent leaves, cities lament the loss and talk about stopping the brain drain. But as Richard Florida, author of *The Rise of the Creative Class*, once told me, "brains don't drain—they circulate." James provides a perfect illustration of this idea. Often the first step out the door is the first step in a circuitous path that leads back home. The lure of home—family, friends, history and the sense of comfort that comes only when we plant our roots in the very soil that spawned us—is a powerful thing. And when talent comes home after the journey, it comes home with experience and greater perspective on the world.

The other lesson that James's actions underscore is the importance of maximizing meaning. As talent circulates, we tend to think that it flows inevitably towards where it is valued most. We flow into the star cities, which are talent magnets where you make the most money, have access to the most amenities and the most appealing lifestyle options. For many people, this remains the case. But as I wrote in *For the Love of Cities*, some choose the option of maximizing their ability to make a difference, to make meaningful impacts in their communities. In smaller, less glamorous cities, we can see and feel the impact of our work. My friend and fellow Akronite David Giffels wrote a whole book on how this notion plays out in Rust Belt cities. He called the book, *The Hard Way on Purpose*, which sums up why we might choose Cleveland over Miami, character over amenities and meaning over money.

James said in his letter, "My presence can make a difference in Miami, but I think it can mean more where I'm from." Very true. In choosing the "hard way on purpose" and going back to his hometown team, James is giving hope to not just Cleveland sports fans and residents of Ohio. He is giving hope to every city that has felt the pain of losing its best and brightest. For every city that has been on the losing side of the talent war, he has shown that there is a pathway to success. If the most talented person in the world in their respective field can choose meaning over money, amenities and other perks, the underdog can win and the Rust Belt has much to offer.

***

On February 14, 2014, the Eighth and Main Tower in Boise, Idaho, formally known as "The Hole" opened to much fanfare and a crowd of 15,000. Ironically, the tower is now Idaho's tallest building.

***

CentrePoint, the stalled development in downtown Lexington, Kentucky, finally began construction on a new ten-story, mixed use office building. Excavation for the underground parking garage began in the spring of 2014, which ended the downtown horse park.

***

Winter the dolphin now has a friend – Hope. Hope was a baby dolphin, rescued near where Winter came ashore in 2005. She was nursed back to health and paired with Winter at the Clearwater Marine Aquarium. They are the centerpieces of the Clearwater travel and tourism economy and were just featured in the Disney movie, Dolphin Tale 2.

***

My hometown of St. Petersburg still has not experienced any meaningful progress on revitalizing its downtown Pier.

End Notes

ENDNOTES

[i] Gill, Michael. "The End of Civic Innovation?" Cleveland Scene, Sept. 10, 2010. http://www.clevescene.com/cleveland/the-end-of-civic-innovation/Content?oid=2120829

[ii] MainStreet. "America's Dying Cities." Newsweek, January 11, 2011. http://www.newsweek.com/americas-dying-cities-66873

[iii] Alpert, Lukas I. "Fort Wayne scratches Harry Baals out for name of government building; goes with Citizens Square." Daily News, March 15, 2011. http://www.nydailynews.com/news/national/fort-wayne-scratches-harry-baals-government-building-citizens-square-article-1.120939

[iv] Waggoner, Martha. "Walk Raleigh: Students Inspire City Campaigns To Encourage Walking." Huffington Post, April 11, 2012. http://www.huffingtonpost.com/2012/04/11/walk-raleigh-campaign-unc-hoboken_n_1418758.html

[v] Ibid

[vi] Garrett, Robert T. "House proclaims Garland as Cowboy Hat Capital of Texas." Dallas News – Trail Blazers Blog, May 2, 2013. http://trailblazersblog.dallasnews.com/2013/05/house-proclaims-garland-as-cowboy-hat-capital-of-texas.html/

ⁱⁱ   Constellation Brands. http://www.linkedin.com/company/constellation-brands

ⁱⁱⁱ   Ibid

ⁱˣ   "Top 25 Arts Destinations 2009." American Style Magazine. http://www.americanstyle.com/travel/top-25-arts-destinations-winners-2/top-25-arts-destinations-2009/

ˣ   "St. Petersburg Voted Number One Arts Destination Three Years Running." May 18, 2012. http://www.stpete.org/news/2012/5-18-2012_st_petersburg_voted_number_one_arts_destination_three_years_running.asp

ˣⁱ   Coleman, Justin. "Muscatine River Monster: The Backstory." https://www.youtube.com/watch?v=TPO4gCnq3vw

ˣⁱⁱ   Sherberger, Tom. "USFSP College of Business study details economic impact of Dolphin Tale. " August 16, 2012. http://www.usfsp.edu/blog/2012/08/16/usfsp-college-of-business-study-details-economic-impact-of-dolphin-tale/

ˣⁱⁱⁱ   Brown, T. Rob. "I am Joplin' mural focuses on message of community." Joplin Globe, Sept 30, 2013. http://www.joplinglobe.com/news/local_news/article_6d8b8566-34ec-5dfa-b789-029fda701fc1.html

ˣⁱᵛ   "Broadway Cars Can Take a Walk." New York Post, February 26, 2009. http://nypost.com/2009/02/26/broadway-cars-can-take-a-walk/

ˣᵛ   Ibid

ˣᵛⁱ   Glick, Justin. "Citing 'Livability and Mobility' Bloomberg Declares Broadway Plazas a Success." Next City, February 12, 2010. http://nextcity.org/daily/entry/citing-livability-and-mobility-bloomberg-declares-broadway-plazas-a-success

ˣᵛⁱⁱ   Sharkey, Joe. "In Salt Lake City; Wide Streets and Conservative Culture." New York Times, August 6, 2002. http://www.nytimes.com/2002/08/06/business/business-travel-ground-salt-lake-city-wide-streets-conservative-culture.html [xviii] McKellar, Katie. "Festival to help rejuvenate Salt Lake's Granary District." Deseret News, June 2, 2013. http://www.deseretnews.com/article/865581032/Festival-to-help-rejuvenate-Salt-Lakes-Granary-District.html

[xix] Ibid

[xx] Jacob Stanley Creative. "Gap Filler, a creative urban regeneration initiative." http://vimeo.com/76843200

[xxi] Ibid

[xxii] Rowe, Peter. "Beer is big, bubbly business in SD, new study confirms." U-T San Diego, April 22, 2013. http://m.utsandiego.com/news/2013/apr/22/beer-big-new-study-confirms/

[xxiii] "Juzcar – The Spanish Village that Voted itself Blue." Kuriositas, December 19, 2011. http://www.kuriositas.com/2011/12/juzcar-spanish-village-that-voted.html

[xxiv] O'Donnell, Christopher. "St. Pete tweaking red light camera system." TBO.com, June 6, 2013. http://tbo.com/pinellas-county/st-pete-tweaking-red-light-camera-system-20130606/

[xxv] Stanley, Kameel. "St. Petersburg to cut red-light cameras by Sept. 30 – at the latest." Tampa Bay Times, March 6, 2014. http://www.tampabay.com/news/localgovernment/st-petersburg-delays-talk-of-red-light-cameras-for-missing-council-member/2168856

[xxvi] "Red Light Cameras Increase Accidents." National Motorists Association.   http://www.motorists.org/red-light-cameras/increase-accidents

[xxvii] "Albuquerque, New Mexico Voters Reject RedLight Cameras." TheNewspaper.com, October 5, 2011. http://thenewspaper.com/news/36/3604.asp

[xxviii] "Big plans announced for 'Boise Hole' ... again." KTVB.com, November 25, 2013. http://www.ktvb.com/news/local/Developers-will-turn-Boise-Hole-into-a--130128033.html

xxix   Edwards, Nathan. "Bank proposes partial fill of Petoskey Point pit." UpNorthLive.com, February 6, 2013. http://www.upnorthlive.com/news/story.aspx?id=857052#. Ui9I-BZDaDF

xxx   Ibid

xxxi   Fortune, Beverly. "Horse farm fence being built around CentrePointe site downtown." Lexington Herald Leader, October 2, 2009.   http://www.kentucky.com/2009/10/02/959668/horse-farm-fence-being-built-around.html

xxxii   Schlueb, Mark. "Inside Orlando's historic Lake Eola fountain, zapped by lightning." Orlando Sentinel, September 6, 2009.   http://www.orlandosentinel.com/news/local/orange/orl-inside-lake-eola-fountain-090609,0,4885508.story

xxxiii   Schlueb, Mark. "We are going to rebuild the Lake Eola fountain better than before." Orlando Sentinel, October 16,   2009.   http://articles.orlandosentinel.com/2009-10-16/news/0910150247_1_dyer-fountain-lake-eola

xxxiv   "Banksy Bashes One World Trade Center In Rejected New York Times Op-Ed." Huffington Post, October 28, 2013. http://www.huffingtonpost.com/2013/10/28/banksy-one-world-trade-center_n_4169568.html

xxxv   Ruth, Daniel. "Dear Mayor: You'll need to self-medicate to deal with the Pier." Tampa Bay Times, February 20, 2014. http://www.tampabay.com/opinion/columns/dear-mayor-youll-need-to-self-medicate-to-deal-with-the-pier/2166565

xxxvi   McCormack, Richard. "A GM Factory With 2100 Workers Closes, And 33,000 Other People Lose Their Jobs – Impacting 120,000." Manufacturing and Technology News, January 12, 2010.   http://www.manufacturingnews.com/news/10/0112/GM.html

xxxvii   "Former GM plant now has five occupants."   City of Moraine, April 9, 2013.   http://www.moraine.oh.us/

index.php?option=com_content&view=article&id=178:form
er-gm-plant-now-has-five-occupants&catid=7&Itemid=111

xxxviii   Rushin, Steve. "The Heart of a City Cleveland Won Round 1 in What Will Be an Agonizing Battle to Hold on to its Beloved Browns." Sports Illustrated, December 4, 1995. http://www.si.com/vault/1995/12/04/208707/the-heart-of-a-city-cleveland-won-round-1-in-what-will-be-an-agonizing-battle-to-hold-on-to-its-beloved-browns

xxxix   "We'll Always Have Love For the City." Pure Detroit, July 19, 2013. http://www.puredetroit.com/index.php/community/well-always-have-love-for-the-city-242.html

xl   Albom, Mitch. "Broke or not, we carry on in Detroit." Detroit Free Press, July 21, 2013. http://www.freep.com/article/20130721/COL01/307200055/Mitch-Albom-Broke-or-not-we-carry-on-in-Detroit

xli   Ken.. "Bike Commuting Continues to Rise." League of American Bicyclists, September 25, 2013. http://www.bikeleague.org/content/acs-bike-commuting-continues-rise

xlii   Murphy, Liz. "Moving Beyond the 'Bikelash'." League of American Bicyclists, December 19, 2013. http://www.bikeleague.org/content/moving-beyond-bikelash

xliii   Schrock, Susan. "Arlington adding bike lanes between downtown and River Legacy." Star-Telegram.com, October 14, 2013. http://www.star-telegram.com/2013/10/14/5244781/arlington-adding-bike-lanes-between.html

xliv   "Editorial: Halfway through term, a solid record for Buckhorn." Tampa Bay Times, March 29, 2013. http://www.tampabay.com/opinion/editorials/editorial-halfway-through-term-a-solid-record-for-buckhorn/2112016

xlv   Brennan, Morgan. "Downtowns: What's Behind America's Most Surprising Real Estate Boom." Forbes, March 25, 2013. http://www.forbes.com/sites/morganbrennan/2013/03/25/

emerging-downtowns-u-s-cities-revitalizing-business-districts-to-lure-young-professionals/

xlvi   "User group discusses future of fairgrounds." FOTO News, July 2, 2014. http://www.merrillfotonews. com/Content/Default/Breaking-News/Article/ User-group-discusses-future-of-fairgrounds/-3/37/7211

Index